MARK

POWER
OF THE
CREED

THESE ANCIENT TRUTHS WILL
CHANGE YOU *and* YOUR WORLD

Copyright © 2019 by Mark Nauroth

All rights reserved. No part of this book may be reproduced or used in any manner without written permission of the copyright holder except for brief quotations in a book review. For more information, please address: info@powerofthecreed.com

FIRST EDITION
ISBN: 978-0-9978918-2-9

POWEROFTHECREED.COM
 powerofthecreed   @powerofthecreed

Editorial development and creative design support by Ascent: spreadyourfire.net

The English translation of the Nicene-Constantinopolitan Creed used in this book and on powerofthecreed.com is published by the Orthodox Church in America. See https://oca.org/orthodoxy/the-orthodox-faith/doctrine-scripture/the-symbol-of-faith/nicene-creed

Unless otherwise noted, all scripture quotations are from the ESV® Bible (The Holy Bible, English Standard Version®), copyright © 2001 by Crossway, a publishing ministry of Good News Publishers. Used by permission. All rights reserved.

Scripture quotations marked (NKJV) are taken from the New King James Version®. Copyright © 1982 by Thomas Nelson. Used by permission. All rights reserved.

Scripture quotations marked (NLT) are taken from the Holy Bible, New Living Translation, copyright ©1996, 2004, 2015 by Tyndale House Foundation. Used by permission of Tyndale House Publishers, Inc., Carol Stream, Illinois 60188. All rights reserved.

TABLE OF CONTENTS

FOREWORD: ARE WE ONE BODY, OR AREN'T WE? 5

1: CROSSROADS 9

2: ENCOUNTERING THE CREED 23

3: WE BELIEVE 37

4: BETWEEN HEAVEN AND EARTH 51

5: ONE LORD 63

6: LIGHT OF LIGHT 77

7: OUR SALVATION 91

8: MADE FLESH 105

9: BORN OF A VIRGIN 121

10: CRUCIFIED FOR US 135

11: ROSE AGAIN 151

12: GIVER OF LIFE 165

13: LOOKING FORWARD 179

EPILOGUE: WHY THE CREED? 195

THE NICENE CREED 197

ENDNOTES 199

FOREWORD
ARE WE ONE BODY, OR AREN'T WE?

"What I'm saying isn't new," the pastor repeated for the second time in his sermon. "Christians have been teaching this forever—at least since the 1980s."

I couldn't help but chuckle.

I was in my mid-twenties at the time and had just started studying the history of the church. This pastor knew many things that I didn't, but there was one truth of which I was certain: *I was born in the 1980s, and Christianity was far older than me.*

You wouldn't know it from the way we do church, however. Changing worship styles, new music, a "fresh anointing," the next generation—almost everything about contemporary Christianity is forward-thinking, ever-changing, and always progressing.

There is nothing wrong with surface changes. Styles come and go. But for all the momentum, we should expect to get somewhere. Instead, the church is stagnant by any objective measure. It may be growing here and there, but not as a whole. Many are abandoning it altogether. And those of us who remain are frustrated, longing for more than tired clichés and pressuring to remain in political lock-step: "Revival is right around the corner" and "This is the most important election of your lifetime."

If hoping for change and fighting culture wars is what Christianity is all about, how has it lasted this long?

In our race forward, we missed something of utmost importance. It's called the past. As in yesterday. And the day before yesterday. And all the days before all the yesterdays right back to when Jesus walked the earth. This entire period, two thousand years of uninterrupted Christianity, is what scripture means when it refers to "the body of Christ"—the church.

But if the church is a body, think what happens when you chop it in two. Or four. Or a thousand. It dies. Even if it is otherwise healthy, nothing can withstand that kind of trauma. Division weakens. Then it destroys.

Now is the time to raise two important questions.

Are we one body of Christ, or aren't we? If we are one body, no wonder we're dying. We're divided. Not just from the church across town, but from the church of the ancient past. We're too focused on what is ahead to pause and look back to the brothers and sisters who went before us. As a result, we spend lifetimes re-learning the lessons previous generations mastered and re-searching revelations they already found.

Are we training Christians to reflect the person and real presence of Jesus Christ in a dark world? If so, why do we spend so much energy pointing out darkness rather than shining light? We win elections and court battles but lose souls in our neighborhoods because our lives don't match up to what we say we believe or, more truthfully, to the Lord we claim to follow.

This book is about putting the body back together again and empowering every believer for action by returning to the fundamentals of the faith that we all share. But be forewarned—unity doesn't mean forcing everyone to believe as you do. Unity requires each of us, no matter who we are or what we think we know, to look back, far back, all the way to the earliest centuries of the church to see how our beliefs and behaviors stack up with the original.

There is power in believing the same thing. In saying the same thing. In doing the same thing. Christians figured this out very early in our history. That is why those who went before us wrote down the faith in *creeds*—carefully-worded statements of faith that held the body of Christ together for the better part of two thousand years. But was it real unity or the silencing of anyone who thought otherwise? Did the creeds capture the essence of the true faith or water it down until there was nothing left to disagree with—or believe in?

Those who dismiss these early creeds as tired traditions, or political propaganda, or relics from Christianity's so-called "dark ages" miss an undeniable fact—the transformed lives of countless men and women who found in such few words a living, breathing expression of the Christian faith.

For centuries, the daily practice of reciting, and more importantly *internalizing*, these creeds ignited in individual believers a passion for imitating the Lord Jesus Christ. And it is the return to these creeds in our daily lives, not just at special times once or twice a week, that will cause us to reflect him from the depths of our being, to speak in his voice, and to act in his ways so that our families, friends, and neighbors may very well say, "He is risen indeed. I have seen him—*in you*."

We need a creed now more than ever. A rallying point. An anchor. A strong foundation. Now is the time to remember what we once knew, to reunite the body and reinvigorate believers, by recovering the purpose and the transforming power of the Creed.

"It is not possible to become a believer other than by raising one's self above the common customs of the world."

—JOHN CHRYSOSTOM

1

CROSSROADS

"Christ in you, the hope of glory."
(Colossians 1:27)

I BELIEVE....

Not I think, I guess, or I suppose.

I believe. These are strong words—and an even stronger foundation on which to stand.

I believe in gravity. Therefore, I get out of bed without a second thought. And never worry about flying off into outer space.

I believe my friend is a true friend. Therefore, I share my heart without fear or holding back, knowing that even my deepest secrets will stay between us.

I believe in God. This is the most reliable foundation that a Christian can stand on. If I truly believe, I step out even in uncertainty, expecting God's light to shine on my path. When I am in need, I call for and count on divine help. When I face temptation or start falling in with the wrong crowd, this belief is the one thing that keeps me steady.

DECISION TIME

As *believers* in Jesus Christ, we face decisions every day that put our beliefs to the test. These are crossroads—big and small.

Ask yourself, *Where does my belief in God stop?* Anyone can believe God in good times, but what if your bank balance is low, or someone does you wrong, or the right thing to do isn't comfortable or convenient or popular? What do you believe then? How will you respond when a loved one hurts you? Or a co-worker lets you down? Or a random stranger cuts you off on the freeway? Do your beliefs make any difference in moments like these?

Who speaks and acts through you then? Do you respond as Christ would, or as everyone else does?

Crossroads like these quickly pass us by. Sometimes we get through the intersection—we make the choice, say the words, or do the deed—without even thinking about it. It's years or decades later that we look in the rearview mirror, so to speak, and wonder: Why did I give in and go this way? Why didn't I tell the truth, take responsibility, and deal with the consequences? Why didn't I stand up for those less fortunate? Why didn't I maintain my integrity—even if only God would know? Why didn't I forgive the one who did me wrong? Why didn't I say something?

Whenever there is a fork in the road and a decision to make, someone is watching. What will they see? Does your life express "love, joy, peace, patience, kindness, goodness, faithfulness, gentleness, [and] self-control" (Galatians 5:22-23)? Would others be able to identify your beliefs on nothing more than the caliber of your character? How would a total stranger describe you? How would you describe yourself?

And what about God? Is he really real to you? Do you know beyond a shadow of a doubt that "he dwells with you and will be in you" (John 14:17)? Or has life gotten in the way and you can't remember the last time you felt his presence?

This is no way to open a book in a feel-good, positive-thinking culture. So be it. What we need most, now as ever, is *believers* who live, speak, and act like *believers*.

Just mentioning the disconnect between what we believe and how we live is treading on thin ice. But I'm not pointing fingers. I'm posing questions that I have struggled with myself. I encounter crossroads every day and want to make the right turns. Though I regularly come up short, my genuine desire is to be a living witness of the life, death, and resurrection of Jesus Christ and—since you've read this far—I'm guessing that is your desire, as well.

How do we get there? How do we live, speak, and act like we believe what we claim to believe? By filling our heads and bookshelves with theologically correct ideas? This is part of what it means to be a Christian. But take a moment to thumb through the pages of scripture and church history and you will discover another level of belief—one where powerful transformation takes place. At this ground-level, foundational to Christianity itself, *I believe* is more than holding a correct opinion about God.

It is passion in action.

WHAT'S COMING

This book isn't about the positions that divide us, the sides we take in debates, or the latest Christian fads. It's about beliefs. Beliefs that change lives and nations. Beliefs that won't break under pressure. Beliefs that were embraced "everywhere, always, and by all [Christians]"[1] since the earliest days of the church.

This book is about the timeless beliefs in the Trinity, Incarnation, Crucifixion, and Resurrection found in our ancient *creeds*.

If you don't know what a creed is, you will by the end of this chapter. If you do know and are looking for all the historical or theological details, this isn't that kind of book. This is a book to read slowly and prayerfully—to ask yourself questions that may not have quick or easy answers. *Why am I not progressing in the faith like I know I should? Why am I still succumbing to the same bad habits? What will it take for me to step beyond myself and really believe?*

The coming chapters are full of the truths that all Christians claim to believe—and, perhaps more importantly, the incredible stories of the men and women throughout history who dared to put these beliefs into practice. Many of them come from times and places very different than our own, yet they encountered the same crossroads that we do. They wrestled with similar fears, prejudices, desires, and regrets. But instead of making excuses or finding the easy way out, they looked inside and settled what they believed in their hearts and minds. Their beliefs changed their lives and the lives of everyone around them.

Here are three of their stories—living proof of the radical transformation that occurs wherever and whenever God and man meet.

SAY "YES"

"Amma!" The little girl clung to Amy's leg. The word meant "mother" or "mommy" in the child's native Hindi. "I don't want to go," she wept.

Amy Carmichael looked down at the girl, who was no more than seven, seeing the desperation in her dark eyes. Preena, like countless other Indian girls in the early 1900s, had been turned out into the streets by her parents who had too many other mouths to feed.

"Go where, Preena?" Amy asked, stroking the girl's black hair, which one of the other missionaries had braided earlier that day. The word *amma* was touching, since Amy was unmarried, and had no intention of starting a family—especially not now while she was working amid the soul-deadening poverty of India's lower castes.

"Tomorrow, my father is coming to take me back."

Amy's stomach fell. Preena's father had sold her to the Hindu temple, where she served as a child prostitute for the pleasure and financial gain of the priests. She had already escaped once and had the scars on her small hands to prove it.

It was the end of the school day, and the children should be leaving, going out to whatever "home" was for them—a tiny flat overcrowded with twenty people, a battered cardboard box in the streets, the street itself. And this was not the first time, of course, that she'd heard stories like Preena's.

Amy felt a surge of compassion. She knew what she wanted to do but was still holding back. This was her crossroads.

Child prostitution was part of the culture—part of the local religious practices, in fact. And she had come here to preach the gospel, not to run an orphanage. What would the leaders of her denomination think? What if they cut her funding? Kidnapping, even with the best of intentions, was against the law. She couldn't take care of Preena from a jail cell. Amy's health had never been good, and she often needed mothering herself. How could she possibly provide the home this girl deserved?

"Please, *amma*," Preena pleaded again.

Years later, Amy Carmichael would write about this crossroads moment in her powerful books, leaving us the witness of the extraordinary transformation that occurred within her.

As she looked down into the face of this child on that muggy, Indian afternoon, it was as if the little girl vanished and, instead, Amy saw the face of Jesus Christ. She could almost hear the words in her heart,

> *Anyone who calls me Lord must leave behind father, and mother . . . and mission board . . . and fear for their own security.*

Years before, Amy had believed the gospel and vowed to spread it to the ends of the earth. Now, unexpectedly, her Lord was looking at her through the eyes of this child, asking,

> *What do you really believe? Do you believe enough to risk it all? Enough to act, even though you're afraid of what lies ahead?*

In the eyes of a seven-year-old child, Amy saw Christ saying, "Here I am. Help me." And though there were many other forces in her life, many choices she could have made, she crossed a no-man's land within herself and simply "believed in the Lord Jesus" (Acts 16:31).

"Yes," she said to the little girl—and to her Lord. "You can stay here with me, and I will raise you."

In those few words and the lifetime of service that followed, Amy put flesh on what she believed. She believed in a way that shifted her concerns from herself to others. She believed in a way that saved her from fear. She believed. And her life was transformed.

There is much more to Amy Carmichael's story—faithfulness in the face of denunciation by fellow Christians, death threats from Hindu priests, a serious injury that left her bedridden and in pain for the rest of her life. But none of that could change what she believed. Over the years, she was a mother to hundreds of children rescued from the sex trade. Her dedication caused India to pass laws forbidding the sale of children. And the Dohnavur Fellowship orphanage she founded on the southern tip of India is still saving lives to this day.

Amy declared, as in the words of the ancient Creed, "I believe in one Lord, Jesus Christ," and it meant so much more than what church she attended. Her belief changed her—and her world.

Is this what you want?

TREASURE EVERYWHERE

Francesco was out for an early morning ride in the Umbrian countryside, trying to get away from it all. The last few months had been unbearable—fights with his family, uncertainty about his future, voices in his head. Maybe the fresh country air would do him some good.

But a few minutes into the ride, Francesco was already looking for a way to turn back. He could hear the faint tinkling of a bell in the distance—a sound that could mean only one thing. It was a warning to everyone within earshot that a leper was nearby.

His heart sank.

Like many in the Middle Ages, Francesco deeply feared leprosy. The suffering, the stigma, the dread of being infected himself. Merely the thought sent shivers down his spine. As the son of a merchant, Francesco would occasionally send donations to the local leper house, but that was as close, he frequently reassured himself, as he would ever get.

Francesco stopped for a moment and watched as a frail figure appeared around a bend in the road. The man's arms and legs were wrapped in loose bandages, and he stared at the ground as he walked. He chanted "Alms, alms" to no one in particular in step with the noisy rattling of his tarnished bell.

Francesco shuddered.

The path ahead was narrow. There was nowhere else to go. So Francesco held his head high, pretended not to see the leper or hear his cries for help, and rode by without a second glance.

He was doing what he always had—lepers were commonplace around his hometown of Assisi—but, this time, Francesco found himself at a crossroads. Call it conscience or guilt, but whatever it was, something made him look back.

"Just give him some money and be done with it," Francesco muttered to himself as he dismounted, removed a few coins from his purse, and walked toward the leper—fighting himself at every step. Things had been different since he left the army, but this was starting to get ridiculous. What was he doing? There were plenty of other Good Samaritans out there. Why did *he* need to get involved?

With heart pounding and head spinning, Francesco dropped the coins in the leper's bandaged hands and was about to turn and run when he paused and saw the man he was helping.

There were fingers beneath the bandages. Furrows along his brow. And the look of gratefulness mixed with fear in his deep, dark eyes. Here was a fellow human being. A brother—not a disease. Made in the image of God, who, like Christ, knew what it meant to suffer pain, ridicule, and rejection.

As the two men stood silently on the road, words from an old Creed Francesco had recited thousands of times in church but had never really understood flooded his mind,

> *God . . . Father . . . maker of heaven and earth . . . and of all things visible and invisible.*

This leprous man had been invisible to Francesco. He saw him on the road, but not truly. What he saw was untouchable, unlovely, and unwanted. Something to be feared, not someone worthy of compassion. But with a simple glance, Francesco's perspective changed. None of that was true. God was the father and maker even of this leprous man—worth so much more than the coins in his hand, or his reputation, or his family name.

Nothing could be insignificant if God made it. No one can be passed by if he has God as his father.

At that realization, Francesco's heart broke and his ego shattered. Maybe it wasn't the leper who needed his help. Maybe it was he who had something to learn.

That was the moment everything changed. With tears streaming down his face, he passionately embraced the man he had been afraid to acknowledge only moments before, kissing his scarred, swollen cheek.

The leper was stunned. So was Francesco. And the rest of the world was about to be.

Francesco is better known to the English-speaking world as Saint Francis of Assisi, and he dedicated the remainder of his extraordinary life to caring for the sick, the stranger, the hungry, and the oppressed. He gave away all he owned, down to his last pair of shoes, because everyone he met took on more value than anything he could possess. All life was a gift to be treasured because it all came from God's hand. He no longer needed "things" to make him feel happy or important. Treasure was everywhere.

What about you? Does what you believe inspire you to see the world and everyone around you in a different light? If not, it can.

PICTURES ON THE WALL

Eight centuries before Saint Francis, an Egyptian prostitute walked into a church. She was there, as one might expect, for all the wrong reasons. Her name was Mary and her habit was to follow young men to the services and persuade them to follow her home. But on that particular Sunday, everything changed.

Mary didn't tearfully respond to an "altar call" or listen to a sermon pointing out all the ways that she "disappointed" God. In fact, she barely stepped foot in the church. Mary's life was transformed when she saw for herself what a transformed life looked like.

The interior of the church was unlike any that Mary had seen before. It was covered in beautiful mosaics that retold stories from the Bible in vivid color. One image in particular arrested her attention—the Virgin Mary holding the infant Jesus.

Even from a distance, Mary could see the difference between a woman who embraced Christ and a woman who didn't. Beauty, love, flesh, even passion—the image of Mother and Child depicted everything with which Mary was so intimately familiar, but it took on a different dimension with Christ in the picture. Here, contrary to all her experience, was beauty that inspired devotion, innocence in the flesh, and passion so pure that it could adorn the walls of a church.

But there was something else in this mosaic—something more than skin-deep. *A holy beauty and purity that came from beyond this world.*

Mary knew *this* world and the part she had to play. Another revealing dress, a little more makeup, a dab of exotic perfume, and she became whomever her lovers wanted her to be. Her allure was the false, fading kind; there was nothing genuine about it. The makeup wore off. The fragrance didn't last. The "love" vanished along with the pleasure. And she knew it.

But the woman holding the Christ child glowed with a radiance that came from within. Christ had actually transformed her—from the inside out. If the picture was to be believed, she shined almost as brightly as he did.

Until that crossroads moment, the difference between Mary the virgin and Mary the prostitute came from the one they embraced.

Can a person really be that pure? she wondered.

She would spend the rest of her life finding out.

Mary entered the worshipful silence of that ancient church, embraced Christ, and went on to become the saint whose life shines down through the centuries as Mary of Egypt. She took the words of the ancient Creed into her heart and life—believing that Christ came from heaven to earth through "the Virgin Mary" and "became flesh." If Christ could enter into the soul of the woman staring lovingly at her from the wall of the church, then Christ could become real and present in her life. And he did.

Mary became an icon herself, of a life changed by the truth that Christ "became flesh and dwelt among us" (John 1:14) and he still comes to live in every heart that surrenders to him. Christ transformed Mary from her core, and her life radiated his glory to the world. Even today, her picture hangs in many churches and her crossroads story is told and re-told as part of the annual preparation for Easter—the celebration of "old things passing away" and "all things becoming new" (2 Corinthians 5:17, NKJV).

When others look at you, who do they see? Someone burnt out, or weighed down, or distracted with the cares and concerns of this life? Or do they see Christ and Christ alone?

CHRIST IN YOU

Mary of Egypt encountered holiness that she couldn't deny. Francis of Assisi found worth where he least expected it. Amy Carmichael heard the cry of her Savior in the plea of a desperate child. Hundreds of years and thousands of miles separate these crossroads moments, yet they share a common theme,

"Christ in you, the hope of glory" (Colossians 1:27).

Christ in Mary made her truly beautiful. Christ in Francis saw what no one else could. Christ in Amy rescued the forgotten and the hopeless. Christ in *you* will change you and your world.

So why doesn't it feel that way? If we believe in the same God and the same scriptures as Amy, Francis, and Mary, why don't we get the same results? Why did their world change while ours remains the same?

There is just one answer: *Our world remains unchanged because we remain unchanged.* We may be in Christ, but Christ is not fully formed in us. He is only in our heads—not speaking in our words and dynamically alive in our actions.

What we need is revival—not in society, but in ourselves. What we need is "truth in the inward parts" (Psalm 51:6, NKJV); beliefs that change everything about us.

Christ can be formed in you and live through you, changing both you and your world. This is the "hope of glory" and the reason for being a Christian. The question isn't *if* Christ can be formed in you—it's *how* that transformation takes place.

In Christian circles, there are three standard answers to this and almost every other question: "Pray more," "read the Bible," and "go to church." These are good habits to have. But I know plenty of people, and I'm sure you do as well, who do all of the above and still look nothing like Jesus Christ.

So what are we missing?

THE POWER OF THE CREED

Someone once said that, "A Christian is an imitator of Christ in thought, word and deed . . . and he believes rightly and blamelessly in the Holy Trinity."[2] For Christians, action and belief are inseparable. If Christ is not evident in our lives, then something we believe about him is wrong.

What then should we believe so that our lives are transformed like Amy, Francis, Mary, and so many others who went before us?

Seventeen hundred years ago, the leaders of the church gathered to discuss just such a question. The debate was intense, but the answer they came to is still repeated to this day. They wrote a *creed*—a brief but complete summary of the Christian faith. Every word was taken from the pages of scripture, confirmed by centuries of experience, and sealed with the blood of those who would rather die than deny what they believed. Their creed became known as the Nicene Creed, after the city where it was written, and was so concise, easy to memorize, and powerful that it was *the* method of Christian discipleship for the better part of two thousand years.

Learning, reciting, and pondering the depth of the Nicene Creed—this is how Christ was formed in the ancient church. And it is how Christ can be formed anew in us.

Whoever said that passion can't be taught was wrong. The Creed contains the gospel in miniature, and as such, it has passed the passion and the power of authentic Christian belief from generation to generation. Single phrases have changed lives and nations. You have read about three of them already. The Creed contains many, many more which we will explore in the next twelve chapters.

The full text of the Nicene Creed is printed in Chapter Two and again at the end of this book. When you read it, it may appear to be more of a problem than a solution. At first glance, the Creed can seem dry, technical, even lifeless. As a child, one of my friends refused to recite the Creed in church and sat down in protest every Sunday because she didn't understand what it meant. Another friend broke into tears one night when the

Creed came up in conversation because it embodied everything impersonal and dogmatic that she resented in Christianity.

But the reality couldn't be more different. If you are willing to dig, to go a little deeper than you have before, to listen to great voices from the Christian past, and allow your thinking to be challenged, then you will discover a hidden treasure in the Nicene Creed. You will find yourself changed. You will find your world changed. There really is power in the Creed, because there is power in the gospel, and that's what the Creed is.

What do you believe? What will it take to change you and your world?

You're about to find out.

"That every person may be able to say, able to hold, what he believes."

—AUGUSTINE OF HIPPO

2

ENCOUNTERING THE CREED

"How then will they call on him in whom they have not believed?"
(Romans 10:14)

I'll never forget the sermon that changed my life—and I only heard the introduction.

The pastor walked up to the podium, set down his Bible, and rustled through his notes for a moment or two. He was about to start speaking on his chosen subject, when he paused, looked straight at the congregation, and said, "You know, it's a privilege even to stand here."

What followed put everything I thought I knew about Christianity on the line.

"It's such a privilege, and I take it seriously. I don't want to teach anything from this pulpit that hasn't been taught before."

I couldn't tell you what the rest of the sermon was about. Those last few words—"anything that hasn't been taught before"—kept repeating in my mind. What did the pastor mean? Was he referring to consistency at his church, or with every church? Ever?

I had heard sermons preached "from the heart" or as "the Spirit led," but, as far as I could tell, this pastor desired to teach from his pulpit only what had been taught in every pulpit throughout two thousand years of church history.

Was he right to approach preaching and teaching from this perspective? I didn't know. All I knew was my ignorance on the matter. I realized that I had no way to tell *if* something had been taught before because I had no idea *what* had been taught before. History had always been my favorite subject, but my interest in the past stopped where the church began. Ancient Israel was exciting and Classical Greece had big ideas. Church history was all funny names and guys with halos—none of which had any bearing on my life, much less my faith. When it came to what the church taught, everything after the Book of Acts and before the Reformation was one big blank.

In the months that followed, I began to study church history simply to fill in the blanks. I wasn't expecting my life to change; I just needed the facts. But as I worked my way back to the earliest days of the church, to Christian brothers and sisters who knew the Apostles personally or were only a few generations removed from the New Testament, what I read shocked me.

The ancient Christian past wasn't just funny names and halos. I encountered men and women who loved the scriptures even more than I did. Most of them knew the Bible by heart, even before it was collected into a single book. I discovered a church that won the culture through force of character, rather than by perpetually fighting culture wars. They transformed empires by the way they lived, while we insist that everyone say "Merry Christmas." But what was most unexpected was the extraordinary lives of ordinary Christians whose salvation meant something more than gaining heaven and shunning hell. They described grace as if it could be lived, not just given at the time of conversion. And they didn't just talk that way—they lived that way. For these believers, righteousness wasn't merely imputed; it was in their blood and muscle and seasoned every word.

The more I read, the smaller I felt. Did I have it backward? Was it my faith, my version of Christianity, that had nothing in common with theirs?

Don't worry. These questions didn't make me "plead the fifth century" and leave my family and smartphone behind for a monastery in the desert. Many have done just that, answering what for them is a sacred call. But me, I live in the same house, drive the same kind of car, and attend the same church that I did before I started "looking back" so many years ago. There were other things in my life, however, that needed to change. Bad habits. Frustrations. Continually feeling burned and burnt out. The answers were right there in scripture, but I couldn't see them through a modern lens. In order to change, I needed a perspective different from my own. My faith was strengthened, and yours can be as well, by the timeless lessons from the Christian past.

COMING TO GRIPS WITH THE CREED

Pick any Christian book from the middle of the fourth century to the early sixteenth century and the Nicene Creed is bound to appear somewhere in its pages. Everyone talked about it—from the biggest names like Augustine,[3] Leo,[4] and Cyril[5] to the less well-known teachers.[6] It wasn't more than a week or two after that fateful sermon that I encountered the Nicene Creed for the first time,

> We believe in one God, the Father Almighty, Maker of heaven and earth, and of all things visible and invisible.
>
> And in one Lord Jesus Christ, the Son of God, the only-begotten, begotten of the Father before all ages. Light of Light; true God of true God; begotten, not made; of one essence with the Father, by whom all things were made; who for us men and for our salvation came down from heaven, and was incarnate of

the Holy Spirit and the Virgin Mary, and became man. And He was crucified for us under Pontius Pilate, and suffered, and was buried. And the third day He rose again, according to the Scriptures; and ascended into heaven, and sits at the right hand of the Father; and He shall come again with glory to judge the living and the dead; whose Kingdom shall have no end.

And in the Holy Spirit, the Lord, the Giver of Life, who proceeds from the Father; who with the Father and the Son together is worshipped and glorified; who spoke by the prophets.

In one Holy, Catholic, and Apostolic Church. I acknowledge one baptism for the remission of sins. I look for the resurrection of the dead, and the life of the world to come. Amen.

That's it. Outside of scripture, these are among the most quoted, discussed, and debated words in the history of Christianity.

If you're already familiar with the Nicene Creed, you may notice some differences between this version[7] and the one you learned as a child or recite in church. For some, these differences are part of the ongoing debate, but for me, I took issue with more than the translation of a word or two.

To be honest, I didn't care for the Nicene Creed the first time I read it. Or the second. Or the fifteenth. For the life of me, I couldn't figure out why the early church was so fascinated by this jumble of run-on sentences. The language was impersonal, especially when speaking of Jesus. "One essence" couldn't begin to describe my relationship with him. The section on the Holy Spirit omitted everything that I thought was important for the unbelievably generic phrase "Giver of Life." And "believe in . . . Church?" Absolutely not. I believed in God, Jesus, and the Bible, but not in a flawed organization made up of people—people who sometimes failed and hurt me.

Perhaps the biggest fault I found with the Nicene Creed was that it existed in the first place. I read the Bible daily, often for hours at a time.

Wasn't that enough? Nothing else should be necessary. The gospel of Jesus Christ is simple, straightforward, and life-changing. The Creed, on the other hand, seemed complicated, technical, and rigid. The textbook example of "tradition."

Paul reminded the churches under his care to "hold to the traditions" (2 Thessalonians 2:15) and "maintain the traditions" (1 Corinthians 11:2) delivered to them, but I didn't know that at the time. For me, tradition was still a dirty word. It meant rote prayers, lifeless rituals, and the kind of self-righteousness that put Jesus on the cross. I wanted nothing to do with tradition.

Or so I thought.

You know that hit song on the radio—the one you can't stand but still catch yourself singing in the shower or humming at your desk? That was what the next few months were like after I encountered the Nicene Creed. I disliked it and tried to avoid it, but, for some reason, it was stuck in my head. I thought about the Creed in the car, at work, at church, and even at the mall. I remember Christmas shopping with my family that December, wandering through crowded stores oblivious to the hustle and bustle, unable to stop thinking about the phrase, "I believe in one . . . Church."

Sometimes the best way to get something out of your system is to just go with it. So I started reading through the Bible, jotting down every scripture I could find related to the Nicene Creed. My guess was I might identify a couple dozen verses. I paused the exercise over a year later after amassing twenty-six pages of references. There were hundreds and hundreds of scriptures, every one confirming the Creed down to the letter and not a single voice dissenting.

2 Corinthians 3:6 calls the Holy Spirit the "giver of life." Why didn't I? Paul wrote in 1 Timothy 3:15 that the church is the foundation on which all truth stands. I believed in the truth, so why not its ground floor? With almost every phrase, the Creed illuminated biblical truths that profoundly challenged my thinking. Instead of assessing it, it had assessed me, and I

wasn't half the believer that I imagined I was. The Creed led me beyond my favorite talking points about God and the Bible to the first principles of a faith far older and richer than my limited experience.

Not long after, I committed the Creed to memory and everything changed. With the Creed in my heart, belief was settled. Wherever I went and whatever I did, everything I believed was in my mind and on the tip of my tongue, ready at a moment's notice. In difficult situations—when feelings were hurt, traffic was bad, or things didn't go as planned—a phrase or two from the Creed would come up from the inside, remind me of what I truly believed, and direct how I responded. When I felt torn between obligations, the fact that there was only "one Lord, Jesus Christ" to honor brought peace. When jobs fell through, money was tight, and things looked impossible, I looked up to and found direction from the one who "ascended into heaven, and sits on the right hand of the Father." Even when I chose poorly and failed to live up to my beliefs, hope in "the remission of sins" and "the life of the world to come" helped me get back on track.

Paul's words to the Romans started to take on new meaning,

> How then will they call on him in whom they have not believed? And how are they to believe in him of whom they have never heard? And how are they to hear without someone preaching? (Romans 10:14)

Belief is prerequisite to everything in the Christian life. Prayer, love, righteousness, even salvation itself—none of it is possible without believing first. With the help of the Nicene Creed, what I believed became part of who I was. The result was that I prayed, and lived, with a confidence that was new to me, but not to the ancient church.

In the fourth century, Augustine commented on the then time-honored tradition of teaching new Christians the Nicene Creed before anything else,

Because [Paul] said: "How are they to call upon him in whom they have not believed?" you have not first been taught the Lord's Prayer, and then the Creed. You have been taught the Creed first, so that you may know what to believe, and afterwards the Prayer, so that you may know upon whom to call. The Creed contains what you are to believe; the Prayer, what you are to ask for. It is the believer's prayer that is heard.[8]

SOMETHING TO HOLD ON TO

Augustine knew what he was talking about. If Christians are weak in the basic truths of the faith, is it any wonder that so many prayers go unanswered, so many of us backslide, and so many pews sit empty every Sunday? These are side-effects of living in the wrong order—of trying to act like believers before actually believing. Of course we struggle with the flesh. The only time we remember that God "became flesh" is at Christmas. We debate the value of human life. And why not? No one told us it is the Holy Spirit who gave it. We're fearful about tomorrow. And with good reason. There's nothing to "look for" or look forward to.

This isn't how Christianity is supposed to be or how it always was. If old habits are dying hard, if you're tired and are ready to throw in the towel, if you genuinely believe but are starting to have doubts, or if you can't seem to keep your head above water—stop everything. Before taking another step or making another decision, you need beliefs that you can hold on to. You need a creed. Augustine said it like this,

> For this is the Creed which you are to rehearse and to repeat. . . . These words which you have heard are in the Divine Scriptures scattered up and down: but thence gathered and reduced into one . . . that every person may be able to say, able to hold, what he believes.[9]

In the pages that follow, we will explore the Nicene Creed for what it is—a short but powerful reminder of what it means to be a Christian. With the Creed in hand, every one of us—no matter where we're from or the church we call home—will be able to "say" and to "hold" what we believe, with powerful results.

BACKSTORY

Before diving into the Nicene Creed itself, some backstory is in order. Where did the Creed come from? Why was it written? Can we trust whoever wrote it? And why has it lasted all these years?

Even if names and dates aren't your thing, you'll find the answers to these questions encouraging. The origins of other historic creeds are shrouded in myth and misattribution,[10] but the Nicene Creed was written at a specific place and time by a specific group of people, many of whom we know by name. We also know their struggles, the strength of their resolve, and how they worked through bitter differences to achieve that result so elusive in the modern world—consensus. The story behind the Creed and the lessons that can be gleaned from it are almost as powerful as the text itself.

The Nicene Creed was compiled in the year 325 at the First Council of Nicaea. This was a formal gathering of 318 bishops and other church leaders in Nicaea, a suburb of Constantinople (modern-day Istanbul) on the Asian side of the Bosporus. It is sometimes referred to as the First Ecumenical Council, because it was attended by a significant number of clergy from both the eastern and western sides of the Roman Empire and because it was an official imperial function, convened by the first Christian emperor, Constantine the Great.

To this day, controversy surrounds Constantine, the Council of Nicaea, and even the Nicene Creed. Some say Constantine wasn't a Christian at all, but rather an inveterate pagan and shrewd political opportunist. Others argue that the Council of Nicaea watered-down Christianity and mixed it with paganism to create "Christendom"—an unholy union of church and state that would eventually give rise to the Crusades and the Spanish Inquisition. There is even the claim that the doctrine of the Trinity was invented by the Nicene Creed, replacing the simplicity of the gospel with Greek philosophy.

In the opposite corner is the religious art, or iconography, that depicts the Council of Nicaea in glowing terms. Literally. All the bishops and the emperor radiate God's glory, with gospel books or crosses in hand, perfectly serene expressions, and halos encircling their heads—some of which are visibly bulging with divine wisdom. Perhaps the only sign of contention in these otherwise idyllic depictions of the Council is a man with a hand over his mouth. This is Arius, the arch-heretic, whom the Nicene Creed silenced once and for all in addition to "cutting off . . . every heresy."[11] It's a happy ending if there ever was one.

Much like the partisan politics of today, the truth about the circumstances that produced the Nicene Creed lies somewhere between either extreme. The Council convened twelve years after the legalization of Christianity and twenty-two years after the Diocletian persecution, the most severe program of violence against Christians officially sanctioned by the Roman Empire. For many of those in attendance, Christianity cost everything—reputation, property, freedom, the use of eyes and limbs, even the lives of loved ones. With the conversion of Constantine, the political winds were turning in the bishops' favor, but it's hard to imagine them selling-out and embracing the very pagan ideas that they had given up everything to oppose.

No, these men were Christians—passionate about protecting the newly legalized church from a different kind of threat: a flavor of Christianity called Arianism that was taking the world by storm.

Arians called themselves Christians but didn't believe that Jesus was God. While this sounds self-refuting today, in the fourth century it wasn't clear which side was correct. If the question of Jesus' divinity has never entered your mind before, then you have the Nicene Creed to thank. To make matters worse, the "Jesus is God" (Orthodox) and "Jesus isn't God" (Arian) parties both seemed to have scripture and popular opinion on their side. The purpose of the Council wasn't to dilute Christianity or to confuse the point, but rather to sort through the noise and get to the truth. If you have ever witnessed a debate on social media between two Christians who don't see eye to eye, you know how messy it can get. Scriptures fly and names are called, but how often are hearts changed or is consensus reached?

Now imagine putting over three hundred of these social media users in the same room. That's what the Council of Nicaea was like. There is a story of the bishop of Myra, Saint Nicholas (yes, *that* Saint Nicholas), hauling off and punching Arius in the middle of open debate. And while it is likely an embellishment of the facts, Santa Claus beating up the heretics illustrates that these were men of like passions, tempers flared, and consensus wouldn't come without a fight. And maybe that's alright. Maybe there are some truths so vital, like the divinity of Christ, that compromise isn't an option and differences have to be worked through until we get it exactly right.

Even after the majority of the Council signed off on the statement of faith that we know as the Nicene Creed, the debate was far from over. Instead of stamping out all heresy, it poured gasoline on the fire. Arianism was alive and well for centuries to come, other heresies cropped up, and in less than sixty years another ecumenical council was held to expand the Creed into the version we know today.

Was the Nicene Creed a failure? If the measure of success was making all Christians everywhere get along, yes, it failed spectacularly. However, Paul told the Corinthians that despite our best efforts at unity, heresies and disagreements will always be a fact of life. "There must be factions among you," he wrote, "in order that those who are genuine among you may be recognized" (1 Corinthians 11:19). As a peacemaker, the Creed fell short. But as a standard for recognizing the genuine from the counterfeit, for dividing between true beliefs and false beliefs, the Nicene Creed has stood the test of time. Seventeen hundred years of church growth, reformation, revival, and even the invention of the internet hasn't produced a more compact, concise, or compelling summary of what makes a Christian a Christian.

The modern world poses many of the same difficulties as the ancient one. The church remains divided on issues as fundamental as who God is, what God does, and how he saves us. There is the ever-present temptation to sacrifice principles for political power. And onlookers still want to know the "reason for the hope that is in you" (1 Peter 3:15).

What will you do when your faith is challenged? What will you say?

You can grab a chair and read the Bible from cover to cover to your unbelieving friend, political opponent, or debate partner. Or you can do what most people do and summarize. Your summary may be genuine and heartfelt, but is it comprehensive? Has it stood the test of time and transformed the lives of millions? Instead of scrambling to find your own words, Paul encouraged each of us to "speak the same thing" (1 Corinthians 1:10, NKJV). Don't shy away from using old words that generations have tested and fire has tried. When push comes to shove, don't be afraid to stand up and confess with multitudes of Christians who went before you, and who will come after you, the words of the ancient Creed.

And never stop putting those words into practice.

DON'T "NOT BELIEVE"

The Nicene Creed is divided into four sections, or articles, about God the Father, Jesus Christ, the Holy Spirit, and life in the church.

If you take a moment to re-read the Creed, you may notice something is missing. The Creed was written in response to error in the church, so why doesn't it specify these errors—the things that Christians *don't* believe? In the official version of the Nicene Creed recorded in the canons of the First Ecumenical Council, a list of heresies immediately follows the section on the Holy Spirit.[12] But in the version taught to new Christians for over a millennium and a half, this list is omitted. Why?

The best way to spot a fake, whether it's a dollar bill or a doctrine, is to know the real thing. We do ourselves a disservice when we focus on what we don't believe to the determinant of what we do. Of course there is a time and a place for polemics, but something is off balance when the church is better known for what it opposes than what it supports.

This extends beyond the public sphere to what we teach. Bickering—let's be honest with ourselves—over grace and law, faith and works, righteousness and condemnation betrays our dirty little secret. We don't expect Christianity to transform us. We expect to be forgiven, not changed. It's easier to rant and rave against what we don't believe than to major on what we do. If what we believed was front and center for the world to see, we would be responsible for it and obligated to live up to it.

This is where the Creed is leading you. Your faith is about to go public. But don't worry. In the next eleven chapters, as we explore the Nicene Creed section by section and phrase by phrase, you'll discover the "reason for the hope that is in you" (1 Peter 3:15) and not the retort for what isn't.

Long ago, a pastor named Leo encouraged his congregation to let the truths of the Nicene Creed really sink in,

> Keep fixed in your mind that which you say in the Creed. Believe the Son of God to be co-eternal with the Father by Whom all things were made and without Whom nothing was made, born also according to the flesh at the end of the times. Believe Him to have been in the body crucified, dead, raised up, and lifted above the heights of heavenly powers, set on the Father's right hand, about to come in the same flesh in which He ascended, to judge the living and the dead.[13]

Why is it important to remember such things? Leo continued, "Relying, therefore, dearly-beloved, on so great a promise, be heavenly not only in hope, but also in conduct."[14]

The result of the Nicene Creed is transformation. A changed life and world isn't just for the faith giants we discussed in the previous chapter. It's for you. If heaven feels a million miles away or you want to do the right thing but sometimes fall short, keep reading. The transformation has already begun. And it all started with two, little words.

"We believe."

*"Nothing can possibly

be done or

remain stable

unless belief precede."*

—RUFINIUS

3

WE BELIEVE

"If you are not firm in faith, you will not be firm at all."
(Isaiah 7:9)

Bill is an entrepreneur—or at least he wants to be. Three years ago, he had an idea for an app that he believed would revolutionize the real estate industry. Since then, he's spent nights, weekends, and a good portion of his savings building a prototype. It's been exhausting work, but Bill knows his idea is worth it. He also knows the balance of his checking account, and without some much-needed capital, growing his side-job into a full-time business is just a dream.

One day, Bill visited an old friend who worked on the tenth floor of an office building downtown. Time flew by, and when Bill realized he was late picking up his kids from school, he quickly excused himself and ran toward the elevator.

He pressed the button to go down, and the doors slid open a few seconds later. Then time stood still.

The elevator was empty, apart from a tall man in an expensive suit. Bill immediately recognized him—he had seen his picture in the newspaper dozens of times. Standing right in front of him, the only other person in sight, was the country's most prominent real-estate developer. This was Bill's moment.

The doors closed, and the floors started to count down. Thirty seconds was all Bill had to sell a total stranger on what had taken him three years to build. He took a deep breath and said, "How would you like to change the face of real-estate for a second time?"

Everything was quiet. Bill was certain the man could hear the pounding of his heart. "What do you have in mind?" he asked, breaking the silence and reaching out to shake Bill's hand.

Good elevator pitches don't happen by accident. Imagine trying to convey your life's work—all the blood, sweat, tears, and eureka moments—with the clock ticking and the adrenaline pumping. Every word counts. What you say could be worth millions if it rings true or stop everything if it falls flat. There are no second chances.

Almost seventeen-hundred years ago, the church faced similar pressures. The Roman world was changing and, while society-at-large still wasn't sold on Christianity, they had at least stopped sending Christians to their deaths in the arena. In the temporary calm, church leaders from the world over met to find the best way to reintroduce their faith to the empire. Many of these men had suffered intense persecution—they knew what Christianity meant to them and had the scars to prove it. But how could they convey all the blood, sweat, tears, and eureka moments to potential converts in a few short sentences?

The church needed an elevator pitch. Hence, the Nicene Creed.

In the centuries that followed, Christianity took the world by storm, thanks in part to these few words lovingly entrusted to men and women eager to leave an old way of life behind and begin afresh.

And how does the Nicene Creed begin? What is the opening line with which the church captivated the hearts and minds of a hostile world? "If you died today, would you go to heaven?" "What would Jesus do?" "God is love." No, the Creed starts much more simply than that; with a statement so brief and so profound that it's easy to overlook.

"We believe."

START HERE

The Nicene Creed starts with belief. So does everything else.

Think about it. A father of four takes a new job in a different city, *believing* it will be better for his family. A college student exercises regularly and spends extra on organic produce, *believing* it will add years to her life. A business executive purchases an expensive sports car, *believing* the added horsepower will boost his self-image. Do any of these people, and millions like them, have a guarantee that their beliefs are correct? No. They may have information that makes one outcome more likely than another, but at the end of the day, people simply believe and act accordingly. Without belief, nothing would get done.

"If you are not firm in faith, you will not be firm at all," (Isaiah 7:9) so said the prophet Isaiah to an unbelieving king. Don't let the word "faith" trip you up. Isaiah isn't telling the king to go to church. He's asking, *Can you believe?* It's a great question—one we would do well to ask ourselves every day. When life feels unstable, like we're walking on eggshells at work or sinking in quicksand trying to make ends meet, pause and reflect, *What do I believe? Do I believe at all?*

Another translation of Isaiah 7:9 goes like this, "If you do not trust, neither will you understand."[15] Is it any wonder then that our modern world, so captivated by all things rational, has more questions than answers? Maybe you have a friend, or at least know the type, who refuses to believe in anything. He lives by "the facts" and thinks faith is a fairy tale. Then tragedy strikes—he loses his job, his daughter is sick, his wife was unfaithful—and you are the first person he calls. Why? Because belief, any belief, is more stable than no belief at all. A house collapses without a foundation, and a runner's feet blister without shoes. Even in a world with terabytes of information at our fingertips, for the Christian, "we believe" always comes before "we understand."

Doubt isn't the opposite of belief—so don't be scared of it. Consider the last words of Jesus on the cross, "My God, my God, *why* . . . ?" (Matthew 27:46, emphasis added). If the Son of God, in his humanity, could ask, "Why is this happening?" should it bother us when we don't fully understand? If those you care about are questioning, or if you're questioning yourself, that's okay. Doubt can be the first, second, or even one-hundredth step in the lifelong journey that is faith. Determine to believe God anyway. Even if everything doesn't make perfect sense, understanding will come. Admitting you don't fully understand won't hurt anything but making a firm decision not to believe will. "If you do not trust, neither will you understand."

In a reflection on the phrase "We believe," the church father Rufinius wrote, "Nothing can possibly be done or remain stable unless belief precede."[16] Nothing. Maybe part of the popular aversion to belief is equating it with a small sliver of life—religion, ethics, politics—instead of recognizing it as the all-encompassing way the whole world works. Farmers plant seeds, *believing* there will be favorable weather and a good harvest. Commuters buy subway tickets, *believing* the train will be on time. Parents pay for piano lessons, *believing* the skills of the teacher will be transferred to the student. Citizens run for public office, *believing* they can make a difference. Far from living in an unbelieving world, you are surrounded by beliefs from the moment you get out of bed.

Rufinius continued, "Nothing in life can be transacted if there be not first a readiness to believe. What wonder then, if, coming to God, we first of all profess that we believe, seeing that, without this, not even common life can be lived?"[17] It shouldn't come as a surprise that God wants us to believe him. If you believe that the alarm clock you picked up at a garage sale for seventy-five cents will wake you up on time, believing the all-powerful creator of heaven and earth isn't much of a stretch.

The Creed goes on to explain what we, as Christians, believe about God. There are profound and potentially life-changing revelations ahead. But before wading into the deep end of the pool, let's take a closer look at what believing is all about.

WHAT DOES IT MEAN TO BELIEVE?

Belief is everywhere. You couldn't escape it if you tried. But anything that ubiquitous is bound to raise some questions, chief among them, *What does it mean to believe?*

Perhaps the best way to understand belief is to determine what it's not. The Nicene Creed begins with the phrase, "We believe," but it didn't have to. Imagine if the first words were,

- » "We reasoned"
- » "We proved"
- » "We felt"
- » "We experienced"

There is nothing wrong with any of these possibilities. Consider the men who wrote the Creed. The bishops assembled at Nicaea were well-educated, perfectly capable of reasoning and debating theology with all the tools of classical rhetoric. They had also proven God's faithfulness time and again through exile, persecution, and threat of death. Their sermons, letters, and poetry exhibit an ardent zeal felt on a deeply personal level. And they regularly experienced their faith through prayer, fasting, sacrament, and miracles that boggle the imagination.

Yet reasoning, proving, feeling, and experiencing are not the same as believing and the framers of the Creed knew this. "We believe" means something more. Consider Daniel, who believed and ravenous lions wouldn't touch him.[18] Or Abraham who believed and fathered a child at age one hundred.[19] Or a certain religious leader who believed and saw his little girl raised from the dead.[20]

This kind of belief isn't about *faith in something* as much as it is about *faithfulness to someone*. Paul wrote to Timothy, "I know *whom* I have believed, and I am convinced" (1 Timothy 1:12, emphasis added). What about you? Do you know God or just facts about God? Are you convinced on an intellectual level or from your core?

"We believe" is an invitation to trust. To find out if God is who he says he is. This isn't something that happens once and then you forget about it. Belief is constant. At any given moment, are you acting like someone who believes? Or does unbelief characterize your day? The more we believe, the more we learn about ourselves. Are we who we say we are? Do we change our beliefs when the going gets tough or do our beliefs change us?

Maybe you're married. Why don't you cheat on your spouse? Is it because you're afraid of getting caught or because you believe in your marriage? If the only thing keeping your pants on is your spouse's watchful gaze, business trips aren't for you. But if you believe in marriage, that belief shapes your actions, thoughts, and desires—even if your significant other is on the opposite side of the country.

Maybe you volunteered for the armed forces. Why? Was it just for a paycheck? There are easier ways to make a buck. There are also less costly means to serve your country or express your patriotism. But if the flag is more than a symbol for you and "life, liberty, and the pursuit of happiness" are more than words out of history book—if they have become higher principles worth believing in and giving up everything for—then the source of such fearless resolve becomes more apparent.

Belief is about dedication and devotion to what you can point to. The Creed reminds us that as Christians "we believe in one God"—that is, not in an abstract idea, but in *someone* very specific.

NOW IT'S PERSONAL

Francis of Assisi, whom we met in the first chapter, knew what it meant to believe in someone.

Francis was the son of a cloth merchant who discerned the call of God as a young man and rejected his privileged upbringing for a life of total poverty. He gave away everything he owned (and some things he didn't) in a sincere effort to live the gospel as he understood it. What started with one man became a movement, and almost one thousand years later the Franciscan Order still follows in his footsteps, caring for the needy around the world.

Not everyone understood Francis—not in his day, and not today. His behavior was always passionate, but often perplexing, especially for those for whom "religion was a philosophy," as G.K. Chesterton put it in his biography of the saint.[21] Who sells everything for a theory? Or sits naked in the snow for a good idea? Or sleeps joyfully in a mice-infested bed for a conjecture? No one. Actions like these only make sense when someone is absolutely in love. "Say, if you think so," Chesterton wrote, "that [Francis] was a lunatic loving an imaginary person; but an imaginary *person*, not an imaginary idea" (emphasis added).[22]

As Christians, we desire to believe the real God, not an imaginary one. But it is a sad truth that those with the most knowledge tend to believe the least. They find themselves unable or unwilling to step beyond what can be demonstrated or analyzed in a spreadsheet. They miss God because they only understand him. Remember, "If you are not firm in faith, you will not be firm at all," (Isaiah 7:9). Even understanding will collapse unless it is backed-up by personal belief. It's not necessary to agree with Francis' exact vision of the gospel, but his heartfelt belief in the person of Jesus Christ is precisely what the Creed means when it says that, "We believe in one God."

Maybe you're struggling to find the same level of meaning Francis did. Maybe it feels easier to believe in your alarm clock than in the maker of heaven and earth. Maybe you've been going to church for decades and feel just as lost as the first day you came. Maybe you've never stepped foot in church before and this is your first encounter with Christianity. Whatever your situation, know this: "Our Lord is to be believed, not discussed."[23] This isn't a call to burn books or drop out of Bible study or seminary. Rather, it is a gentle reminder that God isn't the weather. We discuss weather, sports, politics, art and—more often than not—those discussions don't transform us. But when speaking of God, every word is to be taken personally. God is to be believed—to be trusted and followed as if he were actually present. Anything less and he is no God at all. He is just someone we sing songs and read books about.

ONE GOD

What then should we believe *about* God?

Contemporary society, even some contemporary Christians, say you can believe whatever you want. As long as you're genuine, God is whatever you believe him to be.

The Nicene Creed says differently. God is described in specific terms because he is a specific someone. God is "the Father Almighty, maker of heaven and earth, of all things visible and invisible." He is Father—that means he creates. He created all of heaven and earth, to be precise. Therefore, the universe isn't an accident, and neither are you. In fact, even if you can't see it, God made it. He is Almighty—that means nothing is too out of control for him to fix.

In the coming chapters, we will explore some of these divine attributes in greater detail. But first things first. The most important truth Christians believe about God is that he is one. "We believe in *one* God," the Creed says before anything else.

If someone cuts you off on the freeway, it's good to remember and act in God's fatherly love. If further down the road, your car hits a slick spot and careens into oncoming traffic, knowing God's almighty power could mean the difference between life and death. But what does "one God" mean for you at rush-hour? In fact, what does it mean at all—apart from which religious group you belong or don't belong to? This is where the proverbial rubber meets the road. We need to ask ourselves, *If we can't apply it in everyday life, then why do we say we believe it?*

"We believe in one God," meant something to the men who wrote it.

Think of the world they lived in. It was one of many gods—so many that it was difficult to keep track of them all. What was sacred to one deity was profane to another. When political power changed hands, the gods cycled out as well, demanding different worship from their newfound "converts." Sacrifice to the wrong god on the wrong day and you're done for. With many gods, belief was a moving target and truth was impossible to nail down.

Today, there are fewer gods and goddesses, but is there more clarity? It can be challenging to sort through all the competing voices you read online and contrasting opinions you hear at work or school. Even in church, there is disagreement. Some say God is love and nothing else. Others say he is just and nothing else. Others say he is sovereign and nothing else. Which is it? With so many diverse answers to such fundamental questions, it's easy to see why people are abandoning belief altogether.

That's why when Jesus was asked about the greatest commandment, the guiding principle by which he and his disciples lived, he responded,

> The most important [commandment] is, "Hear, O Israel: *The Lord our God, the Lord is one. And you shall love the Lord your God with all your heart and with all your soul and with all your mind and with all your strength.*" (Mark 12:29-30)

Of all the commandments in the Old Testament, why did Jesus pick this one from the sixth chapter of Deuteronomy? It's not even in Moses' top Ten. True, we believe in one God because there is only one God to believe in. But there's more to it than that. We believe in one God who is "the same yesterday, today, and forever" (Hebrews 13:8). He's consistent and that consistency is contagious.

One God means one truth—one set of beliefs, one code to live by, one standard to live up to. How can we make sense of this sometimes-crazy world? How can we sort through all the noise and get to the heart of the matter? By believing in one God who isn't bound by which party is in power or which country you call home. He was, is, and always will be the same, eternal God.

This should cause you to breathe a huge sigh of relief. The pressure is off. No more figuring out the right thing to do based on potential outcomes or which side of history you're on. What is true when you go to bed, will be true when you wake up. What is right will always be right. "We believe in one God," and because we do, we're stable even when life's chaotic events are destabilizing.

We believe, even when money is tight, that there is a provider who cares for us and our needs.[24] We believe, when a diagnosis is unfavorable, that the one we trust is able to keep our souls in perfect peace[25] regardless of what happens to our bodies. We believe that, even when our chosen political party or ideology is not in power, God is still in charge of history.[26] We believe that by welcoming the stranger and the alien, caring for the widows and orphans, we are somehow entertaining and caring for God himself.[27]

What does all this mean for you on your morning commute? It's more than putting a Jesus fish on your back bumper. One God means consistency. When you believe in one God and let his unchanging nature rub off on you, you're the same person no matter what life brings your way. Open road or bumper-to-bumper traffic, uphill or downhill, rain or shine, the same God rules in heaven and in your heart. If this doesn't describe you right now, that's okay. Just take inventory of the number of gods in your life.

BELIEVING ANYWAY

"We believe in one God." These five words can clear up many of life's stickiest problems—but not all. Why is there evil in the world? Why do innocent people suffer? Where is God in times of war, national disaster, or personal tragedy? Questions like these are easier to answer if there is another god to point fingers at. But "we believe in one God" and don't have that luxury.

This is where many sincere people lose their faith. They come to the edge of themselves—to questions they can't answer or situations they don't understand—and stop believing altogether. I ran into one such person on a late-night flight to Omaha.

Most of the other passengers were asleep. But a man and woman in my row were having a conversation that was hard to not overhear in the hushed cabin. The man was a scientist; the woman was a school teacher.

The scientist did most of the talking. He started by explaining his work developing life-saving medicine. His passion was evident, and the school teacher expressed genuine interest in what he was saying. Then the scientist's tone changed as he began to share his life story with the total stranger sitting next to him. He was raised Catholic and often attended Mass as a child, but his father cheated on his mother and their family was torn apart. He traveled the world, searching for answers from monks, religious gurus, and anyone who would give him the time of day. This pilgrimage made him wiser in his own estimation but didn't satisfy the restlessness in his heart. He tried to be a good person, but nothing worked. His wife left him, he lost custody of his children, his name was dragged through the dirt, his career collapsed, and his bills piled to the ceiling. All he wanted was to be at peace, but it was as if the universe itself was against him.

The school teacher searched for words. "It was a pleasure to meet you," was all she could muster as the plane touched down.

In the commotion after landing, I was unable to speak with the man but desperately wanted to ask him if he remembered the Creed he recited at Mass as a child. If the scientist had taken the words "We believe in one God" to heart, instead of believing a little bit of this and a little bit of that, could tragedy have been avoided? It's hard to say. What is more certain is that with belief settled, the wreck of a man on the flight that night would not have existed. He still may have had unanswered questions. He still may have gone through hard times. But he wouldn't be wondering and wandering, drowning in a sea of competing worldviews.

Your belief in God will be challenged. Don't run from it—run toward it. Even if you haven't figured everything out, believe first. Understanding will come.

Peter beautifully expressed the unwavering belief all Christians share in one of his letters, "Though you have not seen him, you love him. Though you do not now see him, you believe in him and rejoice" (1 Peter 1:8).

"We believe in one God"—this is the foundation on which the Nicene Creed, and Christianity itself, rests. But what does the one God do? And what do his actions mean for us? The answer is coming next.

"We possess the body

from the earth

and the spirit from heaven,

we ourselves

are earth and heaven."

—CYPRIAN OF CARTHAGE

4

BETWEEN HEAVEN AND EARTH

"We look not to the things that are seen but to the things that are unseen. For the things that are seen are transient, but the things that are unseen are eternal." (2 Corinthians 4:18)

Look around you.

No matter where you are, everything was created by God. *Everything.* Even if you are at a cafe in the middle of a large city, your surroundings aren't man-made. God fashioned the iron in the building, the wood of the table, the electricity powering the lights, and even your fellow patrons sipping their favorite coffee.

At least, that's how the Nicene Creed views the world.

As we saw in the previous chapter, the Creed begins with a simple declaration of faith, "We believe in one God, the Father Almighty." From this statement, we know who God is, but what does he do? Is he a present Father or an absent one? Does he use his power to rule by rules or to govern compassionately? Our view of God is more than the sum of his parts; it also includes our understanding of what he does and how he acts. The Nicene Creed emphasizes one of God's actions before everything else,

We believe in one God, the Father Almighty, maker of heaven and earth, of all things visible and invisible.

What does God do? First and foremost, he creates. What does God create? You, me, and everything else in the universe we call home.

BIG QUESTIONS—A LOT OF THEM

The more you allow this first phrase of the Creed to sink in, the more questions it raises. Table the scientific objections for a moment. If God is the "maker of heaven and earth," why are they such different places? Heaven is paradise and earth . . . isn't. If God created "all things," why do things fall apart? Shouldn't a universe created by God always make sense? If God made both the "visible and invisible," does he have something to hide? Why not reveal it all? Then everyone would believe.

Questions like these deserve more than stock answers. "Sin messed up God's plan." "We'll figure it all out when we get to heaven." "God works in mysterious ways." Such sentiments may be sincere, but they are inadequate in the face of hardship and personal crisis. These are the kinds of beliefs that we "smile at, rather than hold fast," Augustine wrote.[28] But it's no laughing matter when people leave church, or never consider it in the first place, because they can't find real answers to life's real problems.

The faith summarized in the Nicene Creed is meant to be held, repeated, and lived to the fullest. So how do we square what it insists about heaven, earth, and everything in between with our everyday experiences? As we explore the phrase "maker of heaven and earth, of all things visible and invisible" an entirely new perspective will emerge, one which will transform not only the way you view God's big, wide world, but the way you make hard decisions, cope with tragedy or loss, and even how you see that person who stares back in the mirror every morning.

God made everything and that changes everything.

HEAVEN *AND* EARTH

"In the beginning, God created the heavens and the earth" (Genesis 1:1). Both were very good—but the earth didn't stay that way. It wasn't long before "the wickedness of man was great in the earth;" so great that "the Lord regretted that he had made man . . . and it grieved him to his heart" (Genesis 6:5-6).

What happened? How could a perfect world created by a perfect God get so messed up?

We all know the story of Adam and Eve—how the first man and woman disobeyed God's command by eating the forbidden fruit. But their disobedience was more than petty theft of God's personal property. *It was a choice between heaven and earth.* Given the option of God or his creation, Adam and Eve preferred creation. Not that there was anything wrong with what God had made. Everything was good—even the forbidden fruit[29]—but not so good as to replace God himself. The original sin was wanting earth without heaven; and today, it isn't that original. We all have to choose between heaven and earth whenever what we want to do is at odds with what we ought to do.

The alarm clock goes off. Will you get up and connect your heart and mind to God and his values through morning prayer and scripture reading—or catch fifteen extra minutes of sleep, then rush off to what's "really" important, like work or school? A co-worker brings donuts to the office. Will you stick with your weight-loss goals to honor the body God gave you—or is jelly filling and satisfying your taste buds just too hard to resist? A loved one dies. Will you believe God in the midst of heartbreak—or become angry, resentful, and never step foot in church again? We tend to think of life and its thousands of little decisions as neutral, but no choice is neutral. Each one is a tug of war between heaven and earth. Faith and values draw us up toward heaven. Most everything else keeps us down on earth.

If we're honest, earth comes out ahead in our lives more than we'd care to admit.

But the other extreme is also possible. When was the last time you heard the term "worldly" used in a positive sense? In speaking of someone great, we may refer to him or her as "too good for this world"—almost as if it's the world that's the problem. "Heaven is my home," the aged preacher says, "I'm just passing through." Really? Then why did God put us here? Why did he create the world in the first place if we were meant to avoid it? The truth is, heaven without earth is just as problematic as earth without heaven.

The Nicene Creed evades falling into either ditch. God is and will always be "the maker of heaven *and* earth." That conjunction should excite you. Because, whether you realize it or not, heaven and earth is what *you* are.

"We possess the body from the earth and the spirit from heaven, *we ourselves are earth and heaven*,"[30] said Cyprian, the third-century bishop of Carthage. Maybe now the conflict between you and your alarm clock makes more sense. "Heaven and earth" isn't about choosing sides because both are inside you, "The spirit seeks heavenly and divine things, while the flesh lusts after earthly and temporal things."[31] But if this sounds all too familiar, Cyprian's conclusion will turn your world on its head. He didn't remain frustrated and defeated in a personal war zone between heaven and earth. Instead, Cyprian remembered who created them both and, for him, that changed everything. "Therefore we ask," he said boldly, "that by the help and assistance of God, agreement may be made between these two natures, so that . . . *the will of God is done both in the spirit and in the flesh*."[32]

Heaven or earth isn't the question—it's a matter of which one comes first. Jesus himself gave us the correct order in the Lord's Prayer, "Your will be done, on earth as it is in heaven" (Matthew 6:10).

TOGETHER AT LAST

Cyprian understood one of the first great truths of the Nicene Creed: *Heaven and earth are compatible.* God made them both. "The heavens declare the glory of God" (Psalm 19:1) and "the earth is the Lord's and the fullness thereof" (Psalm 24:1). As the reality that God is "the maker of heaven and earth" settles in your heart, you'll find your world strangely different. There will still be hard decisions to make. Soft, warm beds and donuts won't magically disappear. Old habits won't immediately change. But the tug of war in your life will become less and less as you realize, like Paul did, that even containers of earth and clay can hold priceless treasure.[33]

Heaven and earth are united whenever you say, "No, I will get up and spend time with God today because he loves me, and I want to love him better" or "No, I will love the body God gave me and honor and take care of it." On your morning commute, at the dinner table, in line at the Post Office—these are the places where heaven and earth can meet. Focus on the small opportunities to make deliberate connections with God throughout your day. As this becomes routine, heaven and earth will work together for you, as they were always created to,

> For the Lord is God, and he created the heavens and earth
> and put everything in place. He made the world to be lived
> in, not to be a place of empty chaos. "I am the Lord," he says,
> "and there is no other." (Isaiah 45:18, NLT)

SHADES OF GREY

The distinction between heaven and earth, up and down, right and wrong, is usually obvious. Helping a grandmother while crossing the street is right. Stealing her purse isn't. But there are times when the lines are blurred, and the right course of action is difficult, if not impossible, to discern. For this reason, the Nicene Creed specifies that God isn't just the creator of heaven and earth. He is also the maker of "all things visible and invisible."

Whenever black and white issues seem grey, or it's difficult to tell which way is up, there is always something we cannot see. Our understanding of God, the world, and life in general is incomplete without venturing into the unseen. The question is, *Are you ready to take the leap?*

While I study the ancient writings of the church because it is my great passion, I write software for a living. Years ago, I ran the technology department for a startup in New York City. For thirteen months, I poured everything I had into a product and team that I genuinely believed in. It was exhilarating work. Then one day the rug was pulled out from under my feet when I was asked to do something that I felt was wrong.

I was born in the Midwest and raised in a salt of the earth church that taught me the difference between right and wrong. My world was black and white until that moment, but amidst the skyline of Lower Manhattan, all I could see was grey. *What should I do?* I didn't have a clue. I didn't even know if what I was being asked to do was wrong per se. I knew it wasn't breaking the law, but there was something on the inside, something entirely unseen, that said, *Don't go there.*

Submitting my resignation the next day was among the hardest decisions of my life. I could always get another job, but letting my team down, losing treasured friendships, and failing to cross the finish line on a project I loved so dearly was a steep price for a feeling. Would I throw everything away for something I couldn't even see?

Yes—and a short time later I understood why. There were other things I couldn't see, they tore the company apart, and everyone went their separate ways not long after I did. I was spared a world of hurt and heartache because I let the maker of "all things visible and invisible" reveal what I couldn't see on my own.

If you want to know the distance of the earth from the sun, a scientist is the ideal person to ask. But if you want to know why a sunset is beautiful, that's a different matter entirely. Some things are real, factual, and genuinely matter, but you can't figure them out on a calculator or study them in a petri dish. Situations like mine fall into this category. If I went by what was visible, I would have overcome my reservations, stayed to finish what I started, and run headlong into pending disaster. It was something much less data-driven that changed my course. So much of life is this way. The friends we bond with, the foods we enjoy, even the jokes we laugh at are determined by factors that aren't strictly empirical. We just know and don't think anything of it. But problems arise when the unseen remains unnoticed or unheeded.

If God is the maker of "all things visible and invisible," then we must train ourselves to see what our eyes cannot. This is a recurring theme throughout scripture, especially in the New Testament,

> You will indeed hear but never understand, and you will indeed see but never perceive. For this people's heart has grown dull, and with their ears they can barely hear, and their eyes they have closed, lest they should see with their eyes and hear with their ears and understand with their heart and turn, and I would heal them. But blessed are your eyes, for they see, and your ears, for they hear. (Matthew 13:14b-16)

> No one has ever seen God; the only God, who is at the Father's side, he has made him known. (John 1:18)

> For his invisible attributes, namely, his eternal power and divine nature, have been clearly perceived, ever since the creation of the world, in the things that have been made. So they are without excuse. (Romans 1:20)

> We look not to the things that are seen but to the things that are unseen. For the things that are seen are transient, but the things that are unseen are eternal. (2 Corinthians 4:18)

Seeing the unseen is what theologians call *revelation*. It's not as spooky as it sounds. Revelation is a kind of knowledge where your confidence is determined by how much you trust the source, not the amount of evidence provided. You can't buy revelation or take a class in it. As we saw in the previous chapter, Christians believe in *someone*, not something. And confidence in someone other than yourself takes time—even if that someone is the "maker of heaven and earth."

Few people believe statements like "My God will supply every need" (Philippians 4:19), "I will never leave you nor forsake you" (Hebrews 13:5), or "I am the Lord, your healer" (Exodus 15:26) the first time they hear them. Our experiences regularly push back against such claims. They seem impossible, but only to our physical eyes and our purely logical minds. When we look with the eyes of our hearts to the one who said these things—to the "Father Almighty, maker of heaven and earth, of all things visible and invisible"—what additional evidence could we possibly need?

That's a rhetorical question. If Christianity has left you frustrated, then you need to take the small step of faith that is a giant leap away from what your physical eyes can see and your human logic can determine.

It is only through faith like this that you can prove God *is*, and that he "rewards those who seek him" (Hebrews 11:6). We seek God by stepping out in faith, trusting that his commandments and directives will lead us, and his power and love will keep us. Far from making our lives a wild goose chase, pursuing the unseen through faith will help us make sense of what we can see.

And yet...

Revelation doesn't mean you will always have all the answers. Life happens. Even when you believe God, there are grey areas—and that's okay. "The secret things belong to the Lord our God, but the things that are revealed belong to us and to our children forever, that we may do all the words of this law" (Deuteronomy 29:29). As you begin to take those first, wobbling steps from the visible to the invisible, focus on what you know, not on all the things you don't. If you're waiting for the answer to every question in order to trust God, you never will. That's why Paul described revelation as knowing what "surpasses knowledge" (Ephesians 3:19). If you stick with what you can see, your world is unbelievably small.

LOOK UP

"I believe! Help my unbelief!" (Mark 9:24). Does this prayer from a desperate father sound familiar? In a sermon on the Book of Hebrews, John Chrysostom explained why so many of us who honestly want to believe, don't,

> Many are the hindrances, many the things that darken, many the things that impede our perception.... With difficulty do we look up, with difficulty do we raise our heads, with difficulty do we see clearly.[34]

When it comes to believing God, the problem isn't that he's unseen. It's that we're looking somewhere else.

In Herman Melville's classic novel, *Moby Dick*, Captain Ahab is frustrated because he keeps getting lost at sea in his hunt for the great white whale. Even with his trusty compass at his side, he finds himself sailing in circles. It served him perfectly well on land, but knowing true north isn't enough to navigate the waves.

Sailors have long used another instrument, called a quadrant, to find and keep their bearings relative to the stars. Ahab resents this. He wants to navigate on *his* terms. And try as he might, he's doomed to wander the open seas until he looks up and surrenders to what the heavens are clearly telling him.

Who hasn't tried to play by their own rules and come up short? Think of the young woman who fell in love at college but ended up pregnant and alone. Or the addict who promised himself that he had everything under control. Or the financial planner who thought that no one would notice if he took a little extra off the top. None of these people started with the goal of wrecking their lives, but each of them came to a point of brokenness because they refused to see the world, or to treat others or their own bodies, as God intended.

When life happens, where will you look? Down—in shame? Out—to those around you for emotional support? Or up—to the God who made you? Even when you believe in God, truly relying on him can be scary. Remember Peter who walked on the water to Jesus but then started to sink when he noticed the wind and the waves?[35] Dietrich Bonhoeffer, the twentieth-century theologian and martyr, beautifully described the freedom—and sometimes the fear—that accompany looking up,

> The disciple is thrown out of the relative security of life into complete insecurity (which in truth is absolute security and protection in community with Jesus); out of the foreseeable and calculable realm (which in truth is unreliable) into the completely unforeseeable, coincidental realm (which in truth is the only necessary and reliable one); out of the realm of limited possibilities (which in truth is that of unlimited possibilities) into the realm of unlimited possibilities (which in truth is the only liberating reality).[36]

This type of transformation doesn't occur with a glance in God's direction—where we quickly acknowledge his presence then rush back to the security of the world we know. It is the result of looking up, long and hard, until the unseen is the first thing we see. "Nor, on the other hand can there be faith," Chrysostom said in another sermon, "unless a man be more fully assured with respect to things invisible than he is with respect to things that are most clearly seen."[37] The author of Hebrews put it this way, "Faith is the assurance of things hoped for, the conviction of things not seen" (Hebrews 11:2). Assurance and conviction don't happen overnight, and when they do, they rarely last. We become convinced day by day as our eyes adjust and our hearts soften to the reality that God is who he says he is—"the Father Almighty, maker of heaven and earth of all things visible and invisible."

This is all that the Nicene Creed has to say about God the Father. But in so few words, the Creed replaces the world we knew with one entirely different. This world begins with belief—not in an idea, but in someone. *In God himself.* There is one God, not many, which means one standard to live up to and one truth to keep us stable. He created everything, from the most distant galaxy to our innermost thoughts, and none of it is so lost that he can't set it straight. In God's big, wide world there are things we can see and there are things we can't. We'll never know everything. But when push comes to shove and reality stares us in the face, we know where to look—up.

And with eyes fixed, we step out in faith, believing *and* trusting. Saying "no" to what we must refuse, and "yes" to what we must believe. We act on what we believe, or our so-called faith means nothing. In the face of life's difficult circumstances, acting on what we believe can be the hardest thing to do. But for the Christian, it is the only wise and reasonable thing to do. How we live, as much or more than what we say, is our witness to the fact that "we believe in one God, the Father the Almighty, maker of heaven and earth."

This is what looking and living up is all about. But Hebrews 11:2 clarifies that we look at someone in particular, and not just in a general direction, "Looking to Jesus, the founder and perfecter of our faith." Here the Nicene Creed transitions from Father to Son. In the chapters that follow, we will uncover timeless truths about Christ's birth, life, death, burial, and resurrection, but not before we see who he is in relation to us—our "one Lord, Jesus Christ."

> *"Let us confess him by our works."*
>
> —CLEMENT OF ROME

5

ONE LORD

"No one can serve two masters."
(Matthew 6:24)

Jesus is God. Every Christian can agree on that, right?

Wrong. Jesus' divinity hasn't always been a foregone conclusion—even for those who read and believe the New Testament. In fact, it was such a hot-button issue that it almost tore the church apart on multiple occasions.

One such instance was the Council of Nicaea. The matter at hand was the teaching of Arius, a popular leader of the church in Alexandria, who believed that Jesus is God—but not in the same way that the Father is God. To our modern ears, the argument sounds like semantics, but the church of the fourth century wasn't about to let it slide. They knew that *if they had Christ wrong, they had Christianity wrong.*

So many of the shortcomings of the church past and present boil down to misunderstanding Jesus. So much of our frustration with "religion" and our struggles with faith are for the same reason. Who is Jesus? Is he God? Man? Both? What did he do? Why did he die? Where is he now? And what should our response to him be? The second article of the Nicene Creed answers these and other pressing questions with remarkable precision,

> [We believe] in one Lord Jesus Christ, the Son of God, the only-begotten, begotten of the Father before all ages. Light of Light; true God of true God; begotten, not made; of one essence with the Father, by whom all things were made; who for us men and for our salvation came down from heaven, and was incarnate of the Holy Spirit and the Virgin Mary, and became man. And He was crucified for us under Pontius Pilate, and suffered, and was buried. And the third day He rose again, according to the Scriptures; and ascended into heaven, and sits at the right hand of the Father; and He shall come again with glory to judge the living and the dead; whose Kingdom shall have no end.

It's a lot to take in at once. Fortunately, we don't have to. The Creed is meant to be repeated, recited, and rehearsed until it grows on us. Or rather, changes us. The second article is the most challenging but it can also be the most rewarding if you are willing to plumb its depths. Nothing can replace the insight gained from decades of reciting these words in their original setting—church—but we'll make the most with the medium at hand and point out the main ideas one by one, starting with the first.

"[We believe] in one Lord, Jesus Christ."

THE ONE AND ONLY

What was your first encounter with Jesus?

Maybe you went to church with your grandparents, and there was an image of Jesus with such a stern expression that you always sat extra straight in the pew. Maybe your best friend from high school called late one night and explained how she "found Jesus" with tears in her voice. Maybe you felt something between awe and dread the day of your First Communion—unsure if you were worthy, or ever could be worthy, of Jesus' body and blood. Or maybe you were downtown and tried to avoid making eye-contact with a man on the street corner shouting, "Jesus is coming soon!" For me, my first memory of Jesus was in a toddlers' Sunday school class. There was a poster with things that were in heaven on one side and things that weren't in heaven on the other. I can still vividly recall the depth of my preschool theology, "If Jesus made heaven, he must be a pretty cool guy."

The gulf between "stern authority figure" and "pretty cool guy" is vast. As is the distance between a transcendent Lord and an immanent one. With so many perspectives on Jesus, it's hard to imagine that any of the preceding examples, or the myriad of others like them, refer to the same God. That's why, before focusing on any one attribute of Jesus over another, the Creed establishes the essential fact on which Christianity itself depends: There is only "*one* Lord, Jesus Christ."

In Chapter Three, we saw what "one God" meant in a world of many gods. But "one Lord" was no less groundbreaking in a world of many schools of Christian teaching, what we might think of as early "denominations." When the Council of Nicaea assembled in the year 325, there were as many versions of Jesus as there are today. They just went by different names. There was the Orthodox Jesus, the Arian Jesus, and the Gnostic Jesus. The Eastern Jesus and the Western Jesus. The Greek Jesus and the Latin Jesus. You get the idea. There could have been as many Jesuses as there were people in attendance, but instead, hundreds of bishops from the world over stood together and boldly professed, "[We believe] in one Lord, Jesus Christ."

The remainder of the Creed didn't make everyone happy—the goal of the Council was to refute the aforementioned Arius, and there were plenty of Arians present—but in the turbulent centuries that followed, the church kept repeating this short, simple phrase.

If you're a Christian, then the Nicene Creed is your creed. Treasure it—especially in situations that can be divisive. Maybe you and your spouse were raised in different churches, and that makes the holidays uncomfortable. Maybe there is a Bible study at your office, but you've been hesitant to attend because the people leading it don't believe quite like you do. Maybe you're having trouble relating to your parents or to your teenaged children because their style of worship is so different from your own. Maybe you've moved to another town and keep comparing your new church with your previous one. These are the times to remember that, as Christians, we believe in "one Lord, Jesus Christ." Don't abandon your convictions, but let the Creed become your common ground.

As we explore what the Creed has to say about our one Lord, you may find yourself in uncharted territory. Instead of turning back for what is familiar, remember that this is the same Lord you've always heard about. All that is changing is your perspective. Before reading on, let the magnitude of Paul's words to the Ephesians settle in your heart,

> There is one body and one Spirit . . . *one Lord*, one faith, one baptism, one God and Father of all, who is over all and through all and in all. (Ephesians 4:4-6, emphasis added)

Now, let's get to know the one Jesus.

CONFLICTING LOYALTIES

The Roman Emperor himself attended the Council of Nicaea; in fact, it was an official imperial function convened at his behest. Can you imagine what went through his mind after hearing his subjects pledge allegiance to one, and only one lord? Constantine is regarded as the first Christian emperor, so maybe he didn't take it too personally, but "one Lord, Jesus Christ" is precisely the kind of revolutionary language for which Christians were put to death a few decades prior.

"Lord" may have been a loaded term back in the day but it's generally fallen out of use today. Especially in the West, we tend to speak of individual liberties and personal freedoms more than lordship and servanthood. That makes relating to Jesus as lord difficult for us. If "lord" is just a synonym for *God*, it's simple enough to have one lord—we discussed how in Chapter Three. But if we define "lord" as *anyone or anything to whom you give your loyalty*, then chances are you need both hands to count the number of lords in your life.

Megan is the top salesperson in her division. Her salary affords a comfortable lifestyle for her family and allows her to give generously to charitable work. Even though she's living the American dream, Megan is still itching for something more. She really wants to "be somebody" and leave her mark on the world. Will her career allow her to do that? If not, is she willing to start afresh and jeopardize the welfare of her family?

Frank has worked in the same branch of a regional bank for twelve years. So when an opportunity for promotion at the corporate office is presented to him, he feels torn. Frank's current job is easy, his co-workers love him, and his family is getting by. The new job makes financial sense, but it also requires uprooting his family to a new town, leaving behind treasured friendships, and mastering an entirely different set of skills. Is the cost really worth it?

Claire is in her second year of pre-med. She enjoys medicine, but she took an art elective last semester and discovered a passion for watercolors. Ever since, she's considered switching majors but is certain her parents, who are both doctors, will not approve. Claire wants to make a name for herself, but she also wants to honor her family's wishes. Can she do both?

There are no clear-cut answers in situations like these, but whatever Megan, Frank, and Claire choose, it will indicate where their loyalties lie. And loyalty to career, friends, family, even self isn't neutral. "You are slaves of the one whom you obey," Paul said bluntly (Romans 6:16). *Slaves*. As in slaves and masters. Servants and lords. Sounds harsh, doesn't it? But if the location of our loyalty determines our lordship, then there is no other way to describe it. We have many lords—and they pull us apart.

A MATTER OF CONSCIENCE

We'll come back to Megan, Frank, and Claire in a moment. But first, a simple question with a serious answer: When making hard decisions, who decides?

You do.

You may ask friends for advice and weigh dozens of opinions, but at the end of the day, you are the one who makes the choices in your life. And that means listening to—sometimes even wrestling with—the voice of your conscience.

There is a story of an old monk whose chronic drunkenness shamed the monastery where he lived. When he died, many prominent church leaders attended the funeral and honored the monk as a saint. The other monks were scandalized by the praise heaped on their late brother and demanded an explanation. They got one—and it cut them to the quick.

The monk's mother was an alcoholic and he was dependent from birth. Every day of his adult life, he struggled to stay sober out of a sincere desire to follow Christ. The other monks saw his repeated failures and judged him on that alone. They missed his progress and, more importantly, his will to change.

Who had Jesus as his Lord? Who was "more" Christian? The repentant monk who actively resisted, but sometimes succumbed to, temptation or the sober monks for whom alcohol may not have even been an issue? The moral of the story is that there is only so much that someone else's actions can tell us about their loyalties—good or bad.

The dividing line that determines whether we are serving "one Lord, Jesus Christ" is rarely as cut and dried as we would like it to be. Scriptures like "This people honors me with their lips but their heart is far from me" (Matthew 15:8) and "Let anyone who thinks that he stands take heed lest he fall" (1 Corinthians 10:12) should give each of us pause. Instead of focusing on outward appearances, look inward to the role *you* play in every decision you make. There are some areas—like not murdering, stealing, or committing adultery—where the decision is made for you, and your part is limited to simple obedience to what your Lord said to do, or more specifically, to what "you shall not" do (Exodus 20:13). But in other situations, like Megan, Frank, and Claire's, the right answer is harder to find, and yet we still must make a decision. How will we? It is these moments where we prove where our loyalties really lie.

In Paul's day, the big, "What lord do you serve?" question was eating meat sacrificed to idols. There was an official pronouncement on the subject from the church in Jerusalem,[38] but years later Paul wrote to the Corinthians that eating or not eating was still a matter of conscience.[39] Earlier in the same letter, when addressing hard questions about marriage, Paul said, "I have no command from the Lord, but I give my judgment as one who by the Lord's mercy is trustworthy" (1 Corinthians 7:25). In other words, Paul didn't always have hard and fast rules to direct his behavior. Neither will you. Sometimes, like Paul, believing in "one Lord" means looking to what you know of God and making decisions for yourself.

It is difficult to understand how conscientious Christians can disagree on issues that matter, like capital punishment, immigration, and even abortion. The reality is that our "one Lord" is also our one judge. "Each of us will give an account of himself to God" (Romans 14:12). And in that day, how will *you* answer your Lord for the actions you took, the decisions you made, and even the "words you spoke" (Matthew 12:36)? Did you choose to serve him? Or were you caught up with the crowd and did whatever your friends, even your *Christian* friends, wanted you to do? Having Christ as your Lord means truly owning every decision you make.

Either you believe that you will stand before your "one Lord, Jesus Christ" or you don't believe that. Now is the time to settle this in your heart.

If you're still on the fence when obligations collide, your lord will be whoever is screaming the loudest or makes the most compelling argument. This is a terrible way to live. You can never please everyone, much less Christ. "No one can serve two masters"—or half a dozen—and "a house divided against itself" never lasts (Matthew 6:24, 12:25).

So what should Megan, Frank, and Claire do? Own their decisions. More important than *what* they decide is *how* they decide. Truly believing in "one Lord, Jesus Christ" means allowing our loyalty to God to determine everything. Paul reminded the Colossians of this in a passage that can be controversial outside the context of Christ's lordship. Stick with it to the end,

> Wives, submit to your husbands, as is fitting in the Lord. Husbands, love your wives, and do not be harsh with them. Children, obey your parents in everything, for this pleases the Lord. Fathers, do not provoke your children, lest they become discouraged. Bondservants, obey in everything those who are your earthly masters, not by way of eye-service, as people-pleasers, but with sincerity of heart, fearing the Lord. Whatever you do, work heartily, as for the Lord and not for men, knowing that from the Lord you will receive the inheritance as your reward. You are serving the Lord Christ. (Colossians 3:18-24)

The final sentence is key, "You are serving the Lord Christ" (v. 24). How? By the attitude of your heart and the way you interact with everyone else.

This truth is liberating. No matter the situation or parties involved, we have one Lord, one loyalty, one person to satisfy, and one standard to live up to—Jesus Christ. Our obligations remain as husbands and wives, sons and daughters, employees and employers, but our loyalty is to Christ first and foremost. It is his opinion that matters and, thankfully, he doesn't contradict himself or change from day to day.[40] As we serve Christ, we are empowered to serve others, becoming better spouses, parents, citizens, and even better human beings as we become more committed Christians.

Don't fall into the trap that Christianity is a zero-sum game—just know where your loyalties lie. On the job, show who your lord is by working hard when others cut corners. On election day, vote your Christian principles, not some party line. When you hit the gym, do it to honor the God who made your body, not just to look good for someone else. Whatever you do, always look inside and ask yourself, *Why am I doing this?* You'll quickly discover that life with "one Lord" is less confusing and more fulfilling than life with many lords ever can be.

TWO SIDES OF LORDSHIP

In his *Commentary on the Apostles' Creed*, Rufinius wrote, "No one is called 'Lord' unless he have . . . a servant."[41] Jesus is Lord of heaven and earth whether or not anyone believes him to be. But he is Lord of your life to the extent you are his servant. That makes lordship a two-way street,

> Why do you call me "Lord, Lord," and not do what I tell you? (Luke 6:46)

> Not everyone who says to me, "Lord, Lord," will enter the kingdom of heaven, but the one who does the will of my Father who is in heaven. (Matthew 7:21)

Verses like these suggest that "making Jesus the Lord of your life" is a process, not a one-time event. Of course, there is a specific moment when the process begins, and that is something to celebrate. But as in a race, the real celebration comes at the end—after running well. Jesus is our lord when we "live as servants of God" (1 Peter 2:16). And servants serve. It's not necessary that they serve perfectly—what waitress hasn't dropped a plate every now and then?—but they serve nonetheless.

In Matthew 21:28-32, Jesus told a parable of two brothers whose father asked them to do some chores around the house. The older brother refused, but then had a change of heart and did as his father asked. The younger eagerly complied, then promptly forgot all about it and did his own thing. When Jesus asked the assembled crowd which brother obeyed, they replied, "The first" (Matthew 21:31). Why? Because obedience is not what is said, but what is done. Whenever you read the Bible, recite the Creed, or sing along to a worship song in the car, ask yourself, *Am I living this or is it just noise?*

But notice how the Creed says that "we *believe* . . . in one Lord, Jesus Christ," not that we're terrified of him. There is a world of difference between following the rules out of fear and following Christ out of love. Anyone with will-power and common sense can accomplish the former; the latter is impossible without being changed from the inside through grace.[42] The "one Lord, Jesus Christ" isn't a tyrannical overlord waiting to smack us across the head the moment we miss it. He is the gentle shepherd of the twenty-third Psalm who exercises his great power primarily for our benefit,

> The Lord is my shepherd; I shall not want.
> He makes me lie down in green pastures.
> He leads me beside still waters.
> He restores my soul.
> He leads me in paths of righteousness for his name's sake.
> Even though I walk through the valley of the shadow of death,
> I will fear no evil, for you are with me;
> Your rod and your staff, they comfort me.

You prepare a table before me in the presence of my enemies;
You anoint my head with oil; my cup overflows.
Surely goodness and mercy shall follow me all the days of my life,
And I shall dwell in the house of the Lord forever. (Psalm 23:1-6)

In this familiar psalm, we see the other side of lordship; one that is often overlooked. Yes, servants serve—but lords take care of the rest. Historically, it was the master who provided food, shelter, healthcare, income, military protection, education, and even political power for his servants. In fact, it wasn't uncommon for servants of wealthy individuals to have more benefits than free citizens. Sometimes they became kings in their own right.

There once was an Armenian prince who appeared before the Roman Emperor Nero and declared himself to be the emperor's slave. Upon hearing this, Nero didn't put the prince in irons or send him to do heavy labor on one of his estates. Instead, he replied,

> Well hast thou done to come hither in person, that meeting me face to face thou mightest enjoy my grace. For what neither thy father left thee nor thy brothers gave and preserved for thee, this do I grant thee. King of Armenia I now declare thee, that both thou and they may understand that I have power to take away kingdoms and to bestow them.[43]

Nero's pride was legendary, but he did what powerful masters do. He gave his servant a crown and made him like himself. Our "one Lord, Jesus Christ" is the "Lord of lords and King of kings" (Revelation 17:14), and we, as his servants, get to be like him.[44] The kingdom we inherit is much better than anything Nero could bestow[45] and the crowns we receive never fade.[46]

Maybe this is why the apostles were so eager to identify themselves as servants of the "one Lord, Jesus Christ." It's how so many of their letters begin: "Paul, a *servant* of Christ" (Romans 1:1), "James, a *servant* of God"

(James 1:1), "Simeon Peter, a *servant* and apostle of Jesus Christ" (2 Peter 1:1), "Jude, a *servant* of Jesus Christ" (Jude 1:1), and "his *servant* John" (Revelation 1:1).

What about you? Are you a self-made man or woman and proud of it? Or are you willing to submit to Christ's benevolent lordship and identify yourself as his servant before anything else? "If you try to hang on to your life, you will lose it," Jesus said, "But if you give up your life for my sake, you will save it" (Matthew 16:25, NLT).

HELP!

Giving up your life doesn't mean becoming a martyr in the physical sense. At least, not for most of us living in the relative security of the West. Here, giving up our lives means entrusting *every aspect of our lives* to God. If Jesus is to be our "one Lord" as the Creed says, then we *must* trust him.

How do you know if you're trusting God? Your first reaction when things don't go as planned is a reliable indicator. Do you rage out? Do you spiral into depression? Do you accuse God of failing you? Or do you ask God for help?

"Make haste, O God, to deliver me! O Lord, make haste to help me!" (Psalm 70:1). *Help!* is the prayer of a faithful servant. Don't be afraid to pray it. Relying on God for things big and small doesn't mean you're needy or your faith is weak. It means you have one, and only one Lord.

In his classic book on prayer entitled *Conferences*, John Cassian encouraged faithful Christians to pray Psalm 70:1 as often as they could,

> Whatever work you are doing or journey you are going, or office you are holding, do not cease to chant this. When you are going to bed, or eating, and in the last necessities of nature, think on this. . . . Let sleep come upon you still considering this verse, till having been molded by the constant use of it, you grow accustomed to repeat it even in your sleep. When

you wake let it be the first thing to come into your mind, let it anticipate all your waking thoughts, let it when you rise from your bed send you down on your knees, and thence send you forth to all your work and business, and let it follow you about all day long. . . . This you should write on the threshold and door of your mouth, this you should place on the walls of your house and in the recesses of your heart so that when you fall on your knees in prayer this may be your chant as you kneel, and when you rise up from it to go forth to all the necessary business of life it may be your constant prayer.[47]

This is what believing in "one Lord, Jesus Christ" looks like. To the man or woman who prays and acts like this, Jesus' lordship isn't a theory. It is an all-encompassing reality on which life itself rests. But why is Jesus Lord and why are we his servants? Because, as the Nicene Creed says next, he is no ordinary man or even an extraordinary prophet.

Jesus is God in the same way that the Father is.

"One should

perhaps

call it union,

and not

knowledge."

—GREGORY PALAMAS

6

LIGHT OF LIGHT

"In your light do we see light."
(Psalm 36:9)

"I hate math," Max mumbled under his breath when he saw the score written in red near the top of his algebra mid-term. He studied hard and worked with a tutor twice a week, but somehow his grades were getting worse.

"I'll never get it," he sighed, burying his face in his hands.

Max doesn't hate math per se. He uses it dozens of times a day without thinking twice. What he hates is being in the dark. Something about algebra isn't clicking for him, and the result is frustration to the point of giving up.

For many, belief in God can feel the same. Faith is tested. Prayers go unanswered. The Bible doesn't make sense.

When people stop believing in God or never start in the first place, often it's not due to anger or resentment, but because they don't understand him. Isaac of Nineveh wrote that even the strongest believers will "desist from all effort" if, in searching for light in the right places, all they find is "darkness upon darkness."[48] Put another way, we can know the truth and still give up when the going gets tough if the words of scripture never come alive in our hearts, the light never turns on in our minds, and tomorrow never appears brighter than today.

In Christianity as in life, one thing makes all the difference between those who finish strong and those who don't—light.

Which is why, of all the Nicene Creed has to say about Jesus, "Light of Light" is one of the most essential points to grasp. Take another look at what the Creed has to say about him,

> *[We believe] in one Lord, Jesus Christ, the Son of God, the only-begotten, begotten of the Father before all ages. Light of Light; true God of true God; begotten, not made; of one essence with the Father.*

So many profound truths are condensed into such a compact package. The Trinity, the nature of divinity, and even the mind-bending concept of eternity—it's all here. But let's set aside the technical language for a moment and get to the heart of the matter. The key to understanding this passage, and God himself, lies in that simple, if mysterious, phrase "Light of Light."

Light, or rather *enlightenment*, is what Christianity is all about. If the term conjures up visions of monks on Tibetan mountaintops, rest assured, that's not where this chapter is headed. But if it's true that "God is light and in him is no darkness at all" (1 John 1:5), then to know and encounter God for yourself is to be enlightened.

This chapter is about light—how scripture and the Creed describe the divinity of Jesus Christ. To appreciate what the Nicene Creed means when it calls Jesus "Light of Light," we need to know what "Light" is. And this involves answering one of the most foundational questions about God, *What is he like?*

THE GOD YOU CAN SEE

Defining God is no small task. Often it is where things get technical and the language not only goes over our heads but bypasses our hearts. Instead, let's begin with what God says about himself. What does God do according to the scriptures and what do his actions reveal about who he is?

"And God said, 'Let there be light,' and there was light. And God saw that the light was good. And God separated the light from the darkness" (Genesis 1:3-4). Before doing anything else, God turned on the light so that from the beginning, nothing he did would be secret. The creation of the universe, man's first breath, the very first page of scripture—it all happens in the light of day.

Generations later, as God's chosen people journeyed out of Egypt, he very literally lit their way. "By a pillar of cloud you led them in the day, and by a pillar of fire in the night to light for them the way in which they should go" (Nehemiah 9:12). The uncreated glory of God, usually the subject of praise and worship, was used as a nightlight.

In the Gospels, Jesus restored the vision of a man born blind, encouraging him to believe in the one he had seen.[49] And in the future, Christ will come again in glory; the "brightness of his coming" (2 Thessalonians 2:8, NKJV) putting his enemies to shame.

Was God obligated to do any of these things? No. He could have left us in the dark about the origin of the universe. Israel could have stopped and asked for directions. The blind man could have believed in Jesus without seeing him—after all, "blessed are those who have not seen and yet have believed" (John 20:29). The future could have remained shrouded in mystery.

God didn't have to reveal himself to us. He chose to. *He wants us to know him.* This is why the Nicene Creed can circumvent all the philosophy and summarize God's nature in one word. What is God like? He's "Light"—that by which we see.

LIGHT FOR THE ROAD AHEAD

Try driving at night with your headlights off or walking downstairs in the dark. The corner of the coffee table and the hazard in the road are easily avoided with the lights on, but when you can't see what's in front of you, you're headed for a whole lot of hurt.

As natural light makes sense of the visible world, so the light of revelation provides clarity to navigate the affairs of life. "Your word is a lamp to my feet and a light to my path" (Psalm 119:105). It's not just our minds that are affected by knowing God. All of life is transformed. Every step can be enlightened—informed and directed by the knowledge of who God is. There is nowhere that his light does not shine and nothing that he cannot illuminate. "Even though I walk through the valley of the shadow of death . . . you are with me," David sang (Psalm 23:4). "The Lord my God lightens my darkness" (Psalm 18:28). "For with you is the fountain of life; *in your light do we see light*" (Psalm 36:4, emphasis added).

Who is God? He is the light by which we *see*—not by which we keep our eyes shut. Part of believing in God is having our eyes, and minds, open to the world around us. We look at all the facts and see everything in this big, wide world. But nothing we see changes our view of God. Just the opposite. Our view of God changes how we see everything else.

In *his light* do we see light.

Take David. He spent his childhood worshipping in the fields and what he learned about God in those quiet moments tending sheep caused him to see things in a different light. Time in God's presence so transformed his perspective that when faced with the terrifying reality of a lion, a bear, and a giant named Goliath, another reality shone even brighter in his heart. "The Lord who delivered me from the paw of the lion and from the paw of the bear will deliver me from the hand of this Philistine," David said with unwavering confidence (1 Samuel 17:37). The light of God's presence illumined the way he saw everything and compelled him to take action while everyone else sat on the sidelines in the dark.

What about you? By what light do you see? Are you swayed by the same sources of information as everyone else or have you dared to take God at his word and begun to see things in a different light? Do you need a stable job and money in the bank to "not be anxious about tomorrow" (Matthew 6:34) or are you secure simply because "he cares for you" (1 Peter 5:7)? Do you long for companionship and give your heart away to feel loved or is your self-worth "hidden with Christ in God" (Colossians 3:3)? When you have every right to be angry, do you give whoever wronged you what's coming to them or do you show compassion, knowing that "the anger of man does not produce the righteousness of God" (James 1:20)?

"The light of the knowledge of the glory of God" (2 Corinthians 4:6) shines everywhere. It should affect how you view and react to everything. Has it? Or has it honestly not made that much difference, like leaving a light on in an empty room?

Enlightenment is a two-way street. God reveals himself, and we respond. But sometimes our response is half-hearted or non-existent because we forget just how miraculous knowing God is.

THE GOD YOU CAN'T SEE

The sun is an average of ninety-three million miles from wherever you are right now. But even from such an extraordinary distance, staring at it for any length of time will damage your eyes. There is a level beyond which our physical senses cannot appreciate its beauty. What about our hearts? If God shines "brighter than the sun" (Acts 26:13), how much of him can we handle? Or hope to understand?

> [God] alone has immortality, who dwells in unapproachable light, whom no one has ever seen or can see. (1 Timothy 6:16)
>
> You cannot see my face, for man shall not see me and live. (Exodus 33:20)
>
> No one has ever seen God. (1 John 4:12)

Verses like these make real, meaningful knowledge of God sound difficult if not impossible. Sure, he may have started the universe by turning on the light, but ultimately God is invisible, unapproachable, and unknowable. His ways are so much higher than ours and his thoughts are so much deeper than ours[50] that saying "I know him" feels presumptuous—like drawing picture of the sun and calling it the real deal.

And yet, the same apostle who wrote that God "dwells in unapproachable light" also said, "I know whom I have believed" (2 Timothy 1:12). And the same prophet who was told "you cannot see my face" spoke with God "face to face, as a man speaks to his friend" (Exodus 33:11).

How are these things possible? Can we see God or can't we? Is he approachable or unapproachable? Can we know him as he really is or will he always be just out of reach?

Never one to shy away from paradox, the fourteenth-century monk and theologian Gregory Palamas answered all these questions in a single sentence, "God is not only beyond knowledge, but also beyond unknowing."[51] That is, God may be great and powerful and past finding out,[52] but he wouldn't be almighty if he were unable to communicate himself to his creation.

A God incapable of revelation is no god at all. You were never meant to be in the dark.

As a Christian—someone enlightened through belief in the one God—you know the unknowable. Paul prayed that the churches under his care, and you by extension, would "have strength to comprehend with all the saints what is the breadth and length and height and depth, and to know the love of Christ that surpasses knowledge, that you may be filled with all the fullness of God" (Ephesians 3:18-19). Knowing what passes knowledge and being filled with all God's fullness is mind-boggling enough. But why would Paul pray for the "strength to comprehend" and not just more revelation? Anything that requires strength means there will be resistance—try building muscle without weight training. Knowing God isn't always easy.

At times, God may seem distant or impossible to understand. That's expected—he's God. But remember his promise that "those who seek me diligently find me" (Proverbs 8:17) and keep on seeking him. Maybe reading the Bible is overwhelming. Don't worry. Jesus said that his followers would "know his voice" (John 10:4). Keep on reading, believing that even if your mind is struggling, his words will transform your heart. Is the world around you falling apart? Rest assured that God "upholds the universe by the word of his power" (Hebrews 1:3) and that the one who watches over you "will neither sleep nor slumber" (Psalm 121:4). Keep on trusting him. No matter what.

Many times, perhaps most of the time, what God tells us about himself is hard to believe. Even a statement as basic as "God is love" (1 John 4:8) seems impossible when you consider all the pain and suffering in the world. How could a loving God allow the crazy things that go on around us to continue? Oswald Chambers faced this question head-on in the opening of his book *The Love of God*,

> God is love. No one but God could have revealed that to the world, for men, and we all indeed, see nothing but its contradiction in our own limited world of experience. . . . No wonder the carnal mind, the merely intellectually cultured, consider us infatuated, mere dreamers, talking of love when murder and war and famine and lust and pestilence, and all the refinement of selfish cruelty is abroad in the earth. But, oh the sublimity of the Abraham-like faith that dares to place the centre of its life and confidence and action and hope in an unseen and apparently unknown God, saying, "God is love," in spite of all appearances to the contrary; saying "Though He slay me, yet will I trust in Him." Such faith is counted to a man for righteousness.[53]

This is why "Light" is an ideal way to describe God. You don't have to know why light is the way it is or acts the way it acts for it to change you. The deciding factor if you get a sunburn the next time you go to the beach isn't your ability to explain why light travels at 186,000 miles per second—it's how much time you spend in the sun.

While reason can tell us many things about God, our job isn't to figure him out. It's to spend time in his presence, let him reveal himself to our hearts, and believe his words until they transform us. "His is a greatness too vast for our comprehension but not for our faith,"[54] Hilary of Poitiers wrote in his classic book *On the Trinity*. "Let us assume that God has full knowledge of Himself and bow with humble reverence to His words."[55]

ONE LIGHT, ONE GOD, MANY CHALLENGES

But what about Jesus? Up to this point, we have explored light as it relates to God in general. The Creed is much more specific. It identifies Jesus as "Light of Light" and "true God of true God."

The full implication of these phrases can be difficult to wrap our heads around. We believe that Jesus is God. But we also "believe in one God, the Father Almighty" and in "the Holy Spirit, the Lord, the Giver of Life." Exactly how many gods does the Creed expect us to believe in?

The answer is and will always be *one*. The traditional way of expressing this truth is known as the doctrine of the Trinity. We believe in *one God in three persons: Father, Son, and Holy Spirit.*

Let's look at the Trinity from another angle—using light. In a sermon on the Holy Spirit, Gregory Nazianzus put a unique spin on John 1:9, "That was the true Light which gives light to every man coming into the world" (NKJV). He claimed that this verse could just as easily read,

» The *Father* was the true Light . . .
» The *Son* was the true Light . . .
» The *Spirit* was the true Light . . .

And he was correct. All three options are equally true. Think what this means. In the list above, there are "three subjects and three verbs . . . but a single reality."[56] The *three persons* of the Trinity shine with *one divine light*. "We receive the Son's light from the Father's light in the light of the Spirit . . . it is the plain and simple explanation of the Trinity."[57]

Maybe nothing about the Trinity feels "plain and simple." Or perhaps all this theology seems like an unnecessary obstacle to a personal relationship with Jesus Christ. If that's how you're feeling, remember David's words, "In your light do we see light" (Psalm 36:9). The Trinity is who God is. This is the light that we have.

The Creed challenges us to walk in that light.

Whatever God is or God does, he is always in Trinity. Nothing about him is ever in a vacuum. Therefore, to speak of God's love, justice, graciousness, holiness, or any other aspect of his character without first understanding his tri-unity is to miss him at the most basic level—and mischaracterize him to the world. The Trinity is one of those profound truths that we must ponder, sometimes even struggle with, until it comes alive in our hearts and enlightens our actions. Ignorance of the Trinity lies at the root of contemporary Christianity's most pressing problems. Consider just one—unity in the church.

"The glory that you have given me, I have given to them," Jesus prayed for his disciples, "that they may be *one even as we are one*" (John 17:22, emphasis added). The "we" in this verse is the Trinity. And the "we are one"—so one in action and purpose that ancient church called the Godhead "divided without division" and even "united in division."[58] Here's the catch. "We" isn't the subject of Jesus' prayer. It's "they"—Jesus' disciples. Christians. You and me. Jesus desires that his church would be "divided without division" and "united in division" just like the Father, Son, and Holy Spirit.

Are we?

In the second half of his short but powerful book, *The Mark of the Christian*, Francis Schaeffer examined the issue of unity in the church, or rather, the lack thereof. Schaeffer was deeply pained by the divisions that characterized the church of his day, but his solution wasn't to forgo all differences and force everyone under the same steeple. He understood, like the faithful men who compiled the Nicene Creed so many centuries prior, that *the most powerful witness of the gospel is not mere unity, but unity in diversity*. "When we come to the place where there is a real difference and we exhibit uncompromised principles but at the same time observable love, then there is something that the world can see, something they can use to judge that these really are Christians and that Jesus has indeed been sent by the Father."[59]

Yes, some of what divides the modern church is petty. But we are also separated by matters of conscience and principle, and to abandon these differences for the sake of institutional unity would be to deny many of the truths that we hold most sacred. Here is the challenge facing this, and every generation. Will we, through love and humility of spirit, be able to demonstrate the "difference between Christians' differences and other men's differences"[60] while maintaining integrity and devotion to the truth?

Turn on the news. How does society at large deal with disagreement? By shaming, mocking, ridiculing, vilifying, slandering, stereotyping, disgracing, degrading, demonizing, taunting, and caricaturing those who hold the opposite opinion until not even a quivering shred of objectivity remains and both sides appear more like monsters than men. The facts are irrelevant. There is no compassion, decency, or restraint. The point is to win at any cost. To be right no matter what. On Sunday morning, we must leave all this at the door. This must not, it cannot, be a description of Christ's church. We must be different, especially in our differences.

If we are not, if unity in diversity continues to elude us and we keep back-biting and bickering, unbelievers have every right to point their fingers and demand, "What do you really believe?"

If we believe in one God and one Light, let us prove it to the world by "loving kindness" and "walking humbly" (Micah 6:8), by "bearing one another's burdens" (Galatians 6:2), by not "insisting on our own way" (1 Corinthians 13:4), and above all by being teachable. You don't have to agree with someone completely to learn from them. Christian brothers and sisters with whom I strongly disagree are responsible for some of the most significant revelations of my life—even the sermon described in Chapter Two that inspired this book. Despite our differences, or maybe because of them, I am forever in their debt.

Listen, and not just to the sound of your voice or to those in your circle. Ask questions, desiring genuine answers. Seek to understand why other Christians see things the way they do. You may discover that your weaknesses are their strengths and vice versa. When there is tension, misunderstanding, or animosity, be the first to say you're sorry and offer the right hand of fellowship. "Confess your sins to one another and pray for one another, that you may be healed" (James 5:16).

The Trinity is challenging. Not because the logic is complicated, but because you and I are expected to live up to God's glorious example. As Christians—one body of Christ—we are "the light of the world" (Matthew 5:14). Will we be one light or many? Will we shine for the glory of God or ourselves?

TRANSFIGURATION

"And after six days Jesus took with him Peter and James, and John his brother, and led them up a high mountain by themselves. And he was transfigured before them, and his face shone like the sun, and his clothes became white as light" (Matthew 17:1-2).

The Transfiguration changed Peter's life. At the time he was afraid to even look at Jesus,[61] and when he wrote about the experience years later, there was still awe in his voice. "We were eyewitnesses of his majesty. . . .

We ourselves heard this very voice borne from heaven, for we were with him on the holy mountain (2 Peter 1:16, 18).

"Light of Light" wasn't a theory for Peter. He had seen it for himself. In an instant, a flash, he understood what the New Testament says in so many words. Jesus is "the image of the invisible God" (Colossians 1:15) and "the radiance of the glory of God and the exact imprint of his nature" (Hebrews 1:3). In Christ, "the whole fullness of deity dwells bodily" (Colossians 2:9). "He is the true God and eternal life" (1 John 5:20), only doing what "he sees the Father doing" (John 5:19), so that he could truthfully say, "I and the Father are one" (John 10:30) and "whoever has seen me has seen the Father" (John 14:9).

Peter saw this in a moment, but it took him a lifetime to grasp what it meant. After describing the glory of the Transfiguration, Peter explained how he finally started to make sense of it all,

> We have the prophetic word more fully confirmed, to which you will do well to pay attention as to a lamp shining in a dark place, until the day dawns and the morning star rises in your hearts. (2 Peter 1:19)

For Peter, it wasn't enough to see the light of God in the face of Christ.[62] That light had to dawn in his own heart.

And it did. Church history tells us of the pillar of faith that he became.[63] The disciple who denied Jesus at the whispered question of a young girl fearlessly proclaimed him while suffering martyrdom at the hands of the Romans. His life shined—brighter than any merely human effort could achieve.[64]

But what about us? We weren't on the mountain. We didn't hear the voice or see the light like Peter. Neither did Paul. And yet he wrote,

> We all, with unveiled face, beholding the glory of the Lord, are being transformed into the same image from one degree of glory to another. (2 Corinthians 3:18)

Does your life shine just like Christ's? Neither does mine. But the scandal of the gospel is that it can. If we're willing, his glory can shine ever brighter in us until the day where we "walk in the light, as he is in the light" (1 John 1:7).

How is that even possible on this side of eternity? We will spend the remainder of this book answering that question as we explore what the Nicene Creed has to say about the Incarnation—the Word becoming flesh so that the world could see the light of God's glory and stop living in darkness.[65]

For now, the words of that enigmatic monk Gregory Palamas will have to suffice. In speaking of the light of God's revelation, he wrote, "One should perhaps call it union, and not knowledge."[66] God shines his light in our hearts so that we can be changed. Smarter? Maybe. Brighter? Yes. Just as others can tell how much time you spend in the sun based on the color of your complexion, the amount of God's light you've allowed to sink in and become part of who you are will shine through everything you do.

The goal of revelation is not to define love, grace, or salvation—but to live it.

This is where the Creed goes next. Jesus "came down from heaven," not to get in and get out, but to be united with us forever so that we could shine with the same, glorious light.

"He came in order to redeem and save the whole man."

—AMBROSE OF MILAN

7

OUR SALVATION

"The bread of God is he who comes down from heaven and gives life to the world."
(John 6:33)

"If you died today, would you go to heaven?"

It's the clincher of any "altar call," the de facto way many Christians strike up conversations about Jesus, and summarizes what most of us mean when we say "salvation." Salvation boils down to two things—death and where you go after you die.

Of course, there is more to salvation than that. Forgiveness of sins, loving your neighbor, doing unto others as you would have them do unto you. The list goes on and on. But when a distraught mother fights back tears unsure if her wayward son is "saved," she doesn't mean if he's living for God. She knows that he isn't. Her question is whether she will see him in heaven one day.

Eternity and mortality are real concerns, and rightfully so. If God is "not willing that any should perish but that all should come to repentance" (2 Peter 3:9), we ought to have the same deep and abiding conviction and share the love of Christ with everyone we can. But if going up to heaven is all salvation means for you, the next phrase of the Nicene Creed may come as a shock,

> [We believe] in one Lord Jesus Christ . . . who for us men and for our salvation came down from heaven and was incarnate of the Holy Spirit and the Virgin Mary, and became man.

The Creed reverses the direction. Before taking us up, salvation comes down—*from heaven* to earth.

CHANGE OF DIRECTION

The Nicene Creed doesn't ignore what happens after death. Just the opposite. Its triumphant, final phrase is, "We look for the resurrection of the dead and the life of the world to come." The future is bright for those who believe—but that's only half the story.

In scripture and the Creed, salvation begins with and finds its most complete expression in the Incarnation. In the person of Jesus Christ, God himself "comes down from heaven and gives life to the world" (John 6:33). That life is lived in the flesh. "True God" becomes true man.

From the perspective of the Incarnation, salvation looks very different. It isn't an escape route after death. In fact, it is more about life than death. Jesus coming *from* heaven is what makes going *to* heaven possible.

Maybe this sounds like splitting hairs. "From" or "to" doesn't matter as long as heaven is the final destination. That may be true. But when it comes to getting there—the day to day process Paul called "working out your own salvation with fear and trembling" (Philippians 2:12)—the two perspectives couldn't be more distinct. When salvation comes "from heaven" it means that you and I can have the very life of God at work within us here and now, transforming us into his image, with his character evident in every part of our lives. "He came [down]," Ambrose of Milan wrote, "in order to redeem and save the *whole* man."[67]

In Chapter Two, I described the personal shock of encountering how the early church understood salvation. As a twenty-first century Christian, salvation was one of those truths that I had to talk myself into believing and daily remind my mind and body to live up to. But for the ancient church, salvation and the powerful reality of the Incarnation went hand in hand. Salvation was *someone tangible* who came to earth and brought the life of heaven with him. For centuries, the church taught Christians how to do more than receive that life. They *participated* in it. The resulting confidence, consistency, and everyday practice of righteousness made my own experience of salvation pale in comparison.

What does salvation mean for you? Is it escaping future judgment or experiencing new life? Is it being found "not guilty" for past faults or is it the will and the power to overcome today's temptations? Does it mean becoming more steeped in biblical truth or living more in the character of Christ? To borrow the language of Francis Schaeffer, is salvation about God's holiness or God's love? A balanced perspective must include all of the above, but more often than not, the modern view of salvation focuses on what we were saved from rather than the one who saved us.

Consider how much teaching there is on grace as it relates to sin, forgiveness, and condemnation and how little there is on grace as the empowerment to give generously[68] or to grow in the intimate knowledge of Christ.[69] We need the former, but without the latter, there is little chance of us actually looking like our savior. Jesus didn't just "not sin." He came that the world "may have life and have it abundantly" (John 10:10).

The question is, how do we share in that life?

THE BREAD OF LIFE

A young man stood near the seaside with a small group of his most intimate friends. He hadn't been there for more than a minute or two before a crowd began to gather and rumors started to sweep through the nearby village.

He's here.

The man was nothing special to look at—a carpenter in his late twenties or early thirties. But he had recently started traveling the countryside as an itinerant teacher and had become an overnight sensation. Everyone was talking about him. Some said that he did miracles. Others insisted that even more amazing than the miracles he did were the things he said. No one, not even the prophets of old, spoke like this man did.

Now there was a crowd on the beach. Some were asking him questions. Others wanted to touch him. Everyone was talking and tripping over one another and the scene started to descend into chaos. Then the man held up his hands and a hush fell over the crowd.

He was about to speak.

"I am the bread of life," he said in a loud voice. "Whoever comes to me shall not hunger, and whoever believes in me shall never thirst."

Excited whispers spread across the beach. Someone let out a cheer. Not only was this man a prophet and a miracle-worker, he was also their benefactor. He would provide them with daily bread, just like the emperor did. The crowd erupted with an applause worthy of Caesar himself.

Again the man held up his hands to silence the crowd. He had more to say.

"I am the living bread that came down from heaven. If anyone eats of this bread, he will live forever. And the bread that I will give for the life of the world is my flesh."

For a moment, everything was silent except for the sound of the surf. Then he continued.

"Unless you eat my flesh and drink my blood, you have no life in you."

The crowd began to whisper. The whisper became an angry roar.

What everyone said about him wasn't true. These weren't the words of a prophet—they were the ravings of a lunatic. Came down from heaven? Eat my flesh? Drink my blood? What utter nonsense.

Some laughed. Others turned away and never looked back.

The man stood alone on the beach with his original circle of friends. He looked each one in the eye and asked, "Will you leave as well?"

A DIFFERENT VIEW OF SALVATION

Jesus is a controversial figure, and this sermon illustrates why. The source text is the sixth chapter of John, but when reading it in the Bible itself, we can sanitize the action. We may imagine Jesus with a halo. The crowd must have been full of unbelievers predestined to reject him. Jesus' words make perfect sense because we can skip ahead a few pages and read what he said at the Last Supper. But perhaps the narrative form recaptures a fraction of the scandal behind Jesus' original message: "I am the bread of life" (John 6:48).

Imagine if you were standing on the beach that day and this is all you knew of salvation. What would you think? In this particular sermon, there is no mention of sin, forbidden fruit, sacrifice, the cross, or even that there is anything to be saved from. All you have to go on is a stranger telling you he came from heaven and you won't make it without him. Or more graphically, without eating him.

Most of us would fall in with the crowd and dismiss Jesus' offer without a second thought. It sounds crazy. It is crazy. And yet, this is how the Nicene Creed presents salvation.

Up to now, the Creed has had very little to say about us. Apart from a brief cameo in the opening phrase, "*We* believe," its focus is God the Father and Jesus Christ. Then without warning, the subject turns back to us. Jesus—"Light of Light" and "true God of true God"—humbles himself,[70] comes "down from heaven," and becomes one of us. How? Why? The only explanation is that he did it "for *us* men and for *our* salvation."

Why do we need saving? The Creed doesn't say. What about sin? It isn't mentioned until the second to the last sentence. This may seem like an incomplete view of salvation. By some standards it is. But for all that is absent, the Creed captures the heart of the gospel according to Jesus.

"I am the *living* bread that came down from heaven. If anyone eats of this bread, he will *live* forever" (John 6:51, emphasis added). Here is the salvation story in miniature. Why did Jesus come? To give you life. How is this accomplished? In the same way food gives life to your body. "If anyone *eats* of this bread." That is, through your participation in, and union with, the source of life.

MIXED UP WITH US

Living the life of God through Jesus Christ—this is how the writers of the New Testament understood salvation. Paul wrote to the Galatians,

> It is no longer I who live, but Christ who lives in me. And the life I now live in the flesh I live by faith in the Son of God, who loved me and gave himself for me. (Galatians 2:20)

And John said,

> God gave us eternal life, and this life is in his Son. Whoever has the Son has life; whoever does not have the Son of God does not have life. (1 John 5:11–12)

It is easy to think of eternal life as synonymous with heaven. But reread these verses and you will see that they equally refer to here and now. "The life I *now* live in the flesh," Paul said because for him, salvation was something that he experienced day by day. Today—not some distant tomorrow—is the day of salvation.[71]

This is how the ancient church understood salvation and preached it to the world. Take the following excerpt from a sermon by John Chrysostom,

> We become one body and "members of his flesh and of his bones." Let the initiated follow what I say. In order then that we may become this not only by love, but in action, let us be blended into that flesh. This is effected by the food that he has freely given to us, desiring to show the love that he has for us. This is why he has mixed up himself with us. He has kneaded up his body with ours, so that we might be one distinct entity, like a body joined to a head. For this belongs to those whose love is strong. . . . This is also what Christ has done in order to lead us into a closer friendship and to show his love for us. He has allowed those who desire him not only to see him but even to touch, and eat him, and fix their teeth in his flesh and to embrace him and satisfy all their love. Let us then return from that table like lions breathing fire, having become terrible to the devil, ruminating on our head and on the love that he has shown for us.[72]

Salvation is about God getting "mixed up" with us. He didn't come down, wash us off, and get back to heaven as soon as possible. He wants to know you, not just rescue you. Think of salvation like baking bread—mix the ingredients; add a little heat; and the result is something new, fresh, and life-giving. If your life is "blended into" Christ's, if your body and all its desires are "kneaded up" with his, if your heart is warmed and your eye enlightened by the fire of revelation, then one day you will look in the mirror and realize that you are a "new creation. The old has passed away . . . the new has come" (2 Corinthians 5:17).

Maybe your salvation feels closer to a burnt piece of toast than what John Chrysostom described. Welcome to the club. In moments of shame and regret, remember that bread takes time to rise. Stick with it. Remain connected to the source of life—even when it feels like it isn't doing a bit of good. "Feed upon what he did for you," Augustine wrote, "and you will grow to know him as he is."[73]

Augustine's advice is reminiscent of the adage, *You are what you eat*. Too many fattening foods make us overweight, but healthy choices and balanced nutrition can prevent disease and improve the quality of life, sometimes extending it by many years. Of course, Augustine isn't advocating a new diet. The principle is that no meaningful change occurs with a single dose. Only as you consistently metabolize something will it become part of who you are.

Change comes, first, through aligning our appetites and desires with God's. "Blessed are those who hunger and thirst for righteousness, for they shall be satisfied" (Matthew 5:6). Next, we begin to take our first, wary bites, "tasting and seeing" (Psalm 34:8) by experience if righteousness actually works and if God is who he claims to be. Sometimes we're unsure. Revelation may start out sweet to the taste and we initially want all we can get, then it turns bitter in our mouths[74] as we encounter hard times and are tempted with the many alternatives life has to offer. But if we keep at it, eventually we acquire the taste. We begin to trust God from the heart and see things the way he does. We even start to treat others and respond to circumstances in the same way he would. This is what it means to "*grow up into salvation—if indeed you have tasted that the Lord is good*" (1 Peter 2:2-3, emphasis added). This is how we change.

But it's not how we *want* to change.

We want salvation to be a one-time event where we say a prayer and everything is immediately different. We want drive-throughs, diet pills, and TV dinners.

Such quick-fixes may produce converts, but rarely Christians. A Christian, by definition, is someone who is like Christ. No one is naturally this way—"all have sinned and fall short of the glory of God" (Romans 3:23)—so there is a process that each and every one of us must go through of "growing up into him" (Ephesians 4:15).

Have you ever looked at someone but saw someone else? There is the young girl who acts so much like her father, down to the contours of her smile and the tone of her voice, that she is obviously his daughter. Or the carpenter who, even though he's left-handed, always saws with his right because that's how grandpa did it. He's never even considered switching hands. Spouses treat each other with the same love and respect that they saw at home. Parents eventually realize that they *are* their parents—in the way they balance work and life, instruct their children, or fall asleep every night in front of the TV. This mimicry is usually unintentional but never automatic. We learn by example. We see then do.

We become like whoever we share life with.

The only way to be like Christ is to share in his life. That means more than just reading about him. "You search the Scriptures because you think that in them you have eternal life," Jesus said, "and it is they that bear witness about me, yet you refuse to come to me that you may have life" (John 5:39-40). Consistent Bible reading is one of the best practices that any Christian can develop, and yet it is not the same as sharing in Christ's life. No one learns to swim by reading how to swim. You learn by practicing with someone who knows how.

Peter challenged us to practice. "Become *partakers* of the divine nature," (2 Peter 1:4, emphasis added) he wrote. What does it mean to partake? Partaking is active. It's present-tense. It means continually participating in and being in dynamic communion with God's abundant life until people on the street begin to do double takes. Until they see someone else. "That's how *he* would say it," they marvel. "That's how *he* would do it. He is risen indeed—I have seen *him* in you."

"Therefore be imitators of God, as beloved children" (Ephesians 5:1).

TWO BECOME ONE

"Dearly beloved, we are gathered here today to sign a stack of government forms."

How many weddings have you attended where the pastor or priest began the ceremony like this?

Probably none. Even though paperwork is part of the big day, it's never the focus. Why? Marriage is a legal arrangement between two parties, governed by civil law. If the license isn't signed, witnessed, and delivered to the courthouse, the marriage is invalid in the eyes of the state. Shouldn't we care that everything is in good, legal order?

Of course, but marriage isn't about paperwork. Marriage is about union. Two lives becoming one. And not one for one moment, or one night, but one for a lifetime. That's the reason to celebrate. When the newlyweds leave on their honeymoon, is it the ability to file a joint tax return that so excites them? Of course not. It's union. Real, physical, what-God-has-joined-together-let-no-man-divide-asunder union.

And yet, when it comes to salvation, it's the "tax return" that gets all the attention. The legal benefits of salvation are immense—forgiveness of sins, atonement, satisfaction, righteousness. Each is amazing and worth being genuinely excited about, but none should outshine the point of salvation—union with God. Two becoming one. Not for one moment, or one "come to the altar" experience, but forever. Forgiveness isn't an end in itself. "Walking in newness of life" is (Romans 6:4).

What if we spoke of marriage the same way we do salvation? *Once married always married.* Yeah, you're going to be sleeping on the couch tonight. *Married by faith alone.* Really? At some point, if you love your spouse, you should at least take out the trash.

Even a question like "Are you saved?" can be misleading. I was married in July of 2012, am married today, and will be married to my wife, Jacqueline, 'til death do us part. Likewise, "by grace you *have been* saved" (Ephesians 2:5), "*are being* saved" (1 Corinthians 1:18), and "*will be* saved" (Romans 10:13). Is salvation a past work, a present reality, or a future hope? Yes.

Salvation has been and continues to be a sensitive subject, especially when participation is involved. Having an active part to play in your own salvation may sound like "works"—doing something to earn a spot in eternity. But the Creed is clear. Salvation "came down from heaven." That means it isn't from earth and there's nothing you can do down here to earn it. Or perhaps all this sounds like "sanctification"—the process of growing in character subsequent to, but not necessary for, the experience of salvation. For centuries, Christians understood the whole package as salvation and not just forgiveness of sins. Participating in the life of God is why Jesus came down.

Never stop being grateful for the forgiveness of sins and the promise of heaven, but don't miss the point and the reason to celebrate—sharing in the life of Jesus Christ. *A marriage may be in perfect order on paper, but it will fail to produce new life without real, loving union.* Two lives must become one. Is "your life . . . hidden with Christ in God" (Colossians 3:3) and is that evident in the way you conduct yourself and treat others? Or are the "cares of this life" (Luke 21:34) still weighing you down and holding you back?

Paul wrote to the Colossians, "When Christ who is your life appears, then you also will appear with him in glory" (Colossians 3:4). This is the Good News. This is how far we can share in Christ's life—until we shine like he does. Leo the Great said it best,

> For the Son of God came to "destroy the works of the devil," and has so united Himself with us and us with Him that the descent of God to man's estate became the exaltation of man to God's.[75]

Salvation is so much greater than we think.

SHARE THE LIFE

How do we practically share in Christ's life?

The pages of history are filled with stories of men and women who abandoned their careers, renounced all possessions, lived in miserable conditions, endured shocking cruelty, and even laid down their lives in pursuit of the life of Christ. Ignatius of Antioch, who was martyred by wild beasts in the early second century, said flat-out, "If we are not in readiness to die into His passion, His life is not in us."[76]

While intended to inspire, examples like these often have just the opposite effect. If this is what it means to share in the life of Christ, what is someone with a family of four and a mortgage supposed to do? Here's the truth: For every monk, martyr, or missionary, thousands of ordinary Christians live the life of Christ staying right where they are.

Anthony the Great is one of the giants of church history and is considered the father of all monks. He spent much of his exceptionally long life in the harsh Egyptian desert, devoted to prayer, fasting, and scripture reading. He was one of the greatest voices of his or any generation, inspiring scores of followers.

But one day during prayer, or so the story goes, God showed Anthony his spiritual equal. He lived in the city, not the desert. He never wrote a book or pastored a church. No one knew his name. He was a simple doctor, who gave generously to the poor and prayed faithfully every night. Only a handful of people knew this man, but he demonstrated the life of Christ to each of them as best he could. That numbered him among Christianity's "greats."

No matter who you are, you can share in the life of Christ and show it to your world.

What if instead of telling others about heaven, you decided to show them heaven through the strength of your character, the depth of your mercy, and the intensity of your love? Would your co-workers and neighbors be more or less willing to listen to the gospel when it comes from "clean hands and a pure heart" (Psalm 24:4)?

Saint Patrick, the fifth-century missionary, is credited with bringing Christianity to Ireland. How does one man change a nation? He was said to have prayed like this,

Christ with me,
Christ before me,
Christ behind me,
Christ in me,
Christ beneath me,
Christ above me,
Christ on my right,
Christ on my left,
Christ when I lie down,
Christ when I sit down,
Christ in the heart of every man who thinks of me,
Christ in the mouth of every man who speaks of me,
Christ in the eye that sees me,
Christ in the ear that hears me.[77]

This is the prayer of a saved man—someone for whom the Good News is more than forgiveness and the sweet hereafter. For Patrick or whoever wrote this treasured prayer, salvation meant *identification* with Jesus Christ.

Is Christ in the heart of everyone who thinks of you, the mouth of everyone who speaks of you, the eye of everyone who sees you, and the ear of everyone who hears you? He can be. That is the reason why he "came down from heaven."

And yet, as marvelous as this is, salvation doesn't stop with knowing Christ and developing in his character. It keeps going until even your body is affected. Incarnation—God becoming flesh—is where the real, transformative power of the Creed lies.

"The Gospel faith proclaims the union of God and man."

—HILARY OF POITIERS

8

MADE FLESH

"Unite my heart to fear your name."
(Psalm 86:11)

"Look up," the tour guide encouraged the group I was with as we stepped inside a historic cathedral in the heart of downtown Sacramento. "The dome is spectacular."

The ceiling was stunning indeed—a vast canopy of vivid color—but something else caught my attention. At the front of the sanctuary was a wooden screen adorned with the text of an old Latin hymn. Two words stood above the altar in prominent, gold letters: *VERBUM CARO*.

You couldn't miss it. Everything in the cathedral—the architecture, artwork, even the cross overhead—pointed toward these two words.

VERBUM CARO.

"The Word as Flesh."

There were other stops on the tour, and we moved on after a minute or two. But those few moments in the sanctuary gave me pause. Of all the ways to engage visitors and encourage the faithful, why "the Word as Flesh?" Isn't "Jesus loves you" or "He is risen" more relevant? Of all the events in the life of Christ, why put the Incarnation front and center? What about the Crucifixion or the Resurrection? And if "the Word as Flesh" really is that important, why say it in a dead language that so few people understand?

Like everyone else in that church, I was challenged to slow down and think differently about the gospel.

The importance of the Incarnation—"the Word as Flesh"—to the Christian faith is impossible to overstate. John said that we know God and are confident in our beliefs about him to the extent we embrace this truth and incorporate it into our lives,

> By this you know the Spirit of God: Every spirit that confesses that Jesus Christ has come in the flesh is of God, and every spirit that does not confess that Jesus Christ has come in the flesh is not of God. (1 John 4:2-3, NKJV)

With John's words in mind, take another look at the second article of the Nicene Creed,

> [We believe] in one Lord Jesus Christ . . . who for us men and for our salvation came down from heaven and was incarnate of the Holy Spirit and the Virgin Mary, and became man.

Today, Christians tend to compartmentalize everything. Spiritual and physical rarely meet, resulting in conflicting opinions and warring desires that leave us feeling guilty, shamed, and inadequate.

The Creed says differently.

How did Jesus "come down from heaven?" He "was incarnate." That is, God became *flesh*—the spiritual and the physical met in the person of Jesus Christ and worked together instead of tearing each other apart.

This is the radical concept at the heart of the Nicene Creed. If we miss or dismiss it, we risk turning Christianity into something that it is not—a purely spiritual experience. While remaining everything that God is, Jesus became visible, physical, *human*. If Christ is all these things, then

Christianity must be as well or our faith is incomplete and the gospel loses its transformative power.

God became flesh. That's good news for our flesh.

LIFE OR DEATH

For many Christians, "flesh" is a dirty word—it's what we blame when we lose our temper, sleep-in instead of hitting the gym, or eat the entire bag of candy after intending to have a handful. And so the Incarnation, the inconvenient truth that God became what embarrasses us, is a side note mentioned once a year at Christmas.

For the ancient church, however, the Incarnation was everything. They believed that God became flesh, not to save them from it, but to demonstrate how to glorify him in and through it. Salvation was physical. It was meant to be *embodied*; not just at a historical point in time but every day and by every Christian. Incarnation meant being like Christ and experiencing his life in tangible ways—overcoming temptation, witnessing the miraculous, communing with him in the sacraments, and even suffering for the faith.

The difference between now and then is not our level of dedication or devotion. It is what we do with the Incarnation. It is how we view physicality, the flesh, and life itself. Consider the following scriptures,

> And without controversy great is the mystery of godliness: God was manifested in the flesh. (1 Timothy 3:16, NKJV)

> That which was from the beginning, which we have heard, which we have seen with our eyes, which we looked upon and have touched with our hands, concerning the word of life—the life was made manifest, and we have seen it. (1 John 1:1-2)

> And the Word became flesh and dwelt among us, and we have seen his glory, glory as of the only Son from the Father, full of grace and truth. (John 1:14)

What comes to mind when you read these verses? Those who miss the physical reality of the Incarnation tend to think about *death*. Jesus couldn't die for our sins without "becoming man" first, so the Incarnation matters primarily as a prerequisite for the cross. Its only connection to us is that it was necessary to save us. Jesus was "born to die," as the saying goes.

But when John speaks of *hearing, seeing,* and *touching* the Word made flesh who *dwelt* among us, his subject isn't Jesus' death. It is his *life*—a life that if scripture and the Creed are to be believed, was both fully human and fully divine. The Incarnation is about life, not death. It is about who Jesus was from the moment of his conception even more than the marvelous things he would grow up to do.

So, who is Jesus? According to the Nicene Creed, he is the "true God" who "became man." The God part we can begin to understand and was the subject of Chapter Six. But becoming human—just as human as you and I—contradicts everything we know of God and ourselves.

If Jesus was just like us, then why was his life so different from ours? The ancient church wrestled with this question. Often, they didn't see eye to eye. But the answer they came to and enshrined in the Creed was the secret to their success. If you have found yourself looking back with nostalgia throughout this book longing for a taste of what previous generations enjoyed, then get ready to embrace the Incarnation and all its physical ramifications with the same passion they did.

It's time to know Christ as his earliest followers did—in the flesh—and come to understand ourselves, and our flesh, in the process.

RETHINKING "THE FLESH"

Jesus in the Gospels is unlike anyone you have ever met. He walked on the waves, turned water to wine, died and rose again three days later, and did countless other things that aren't "human" in the traditional meaning of the word. This disparity between the Gospel narrative and everyday experience led many to conclude that Jesus didn't "become man" in a literal sense. Dozens of heresies sprung up in the early centuries of the church claiming that Jesus merely looked like us. He was God in disguise or human in name only.

Others fell into the opposite ditch and believed that Jesus was so human that he couldn't be God, at least not God in the same way the Father is. How could the Eternal be born in time,[78] the Almighty hunger[79] and thirst,[80] or the Impassible suffer and die a humiliating death?[81] This was Arius' argument at the council of Nicaea. Jesus was God in name only.

But those who believed scripture, even when it seemed to contradict itself, weren't about to explain away the controversy by making Jesus anything less than fully God and fully man. "We needed an Incarnate God,"[82] Gregory Nazianzus insisted. Why?

Because God "becoming man" is as much about mankind as it is about God. Paul wrote to the Romans,

> By sending his own Son in the likeness of sinful flesh and for sin, he condemned sin in the flesh. (Romans 8:3)

Another, less literal version of Romans 8:3 reads, "He sent his own Son in *a body like the bodies we sinners have*" (NLT, emphasis added). Think what this means. Jesus' body was identical with ours, yet he didn't do any of the things that we sinners do. Is Paul rubbing Jesus' perfection in our faces? No, he is making a powerful point. *The* point of the Incarnation.

Jesus "was incarnate" but not carnal—that is, not owned and driven by the desires of the flesh. He "became man" without becoming a sinner. Therefore, *flesh and sinfulness are not the same thing*—not for Christ but also not for us.

The classic text for the Incarnation is John 1:14, "The Word became flesh and dwelt among us, and we have seen his glory." Note the progression: flesh *then* glory. Jesus' body was the means, and not the obstacle, to display God's glory to an unbelieving world. What about us? If Jesus truly was "made like his brothers in every respect" (Hebrews 2:17), can our bodies—hungry, tired, and stressed-out as they are—shine with the same light?

The answer is *yes,* and this is why the Incarnation matters. Why do so many Christians struggle with the flesh?

They forget God became it.

BEATEN BY BROWNIES

"I had so much trouble with my flesh yesterday...."

My interest was piqued. I was sixteen years old and waiting in the foyer for church to start. Several women were standing a few yards away and try as I might to mind my own business, their conversation was too intriguing to ignore. *What could she have done?* My teenage mind jumped to the most unchristian conclusions. I knew I shouldn't, but I wanted to hear more. So I took a step closer—eager for what was coming next.

"I had so much trouble with my flesh yesterday. I really wanted another brownie."

Seriously? I sighed. *Brownies wouldn't make the tabloids.*

The sanctuary doors opened, and the conversation broke up as everyone funneled inside. Everyone except me. I stood there troubled. By brownies of all things.

Before you dismiss this event as trivial—it wasn't. Not for me. In the span of a few seconds I had gone from intrigued, to unimpressed, to on the verge of renouncing my faith. You see, this woman with the brownie problem was someone I looked up to. She was a leader in the church and, though I never found the courage to tell her, an inspiration to me. She was the best Christian I knew.

But from what I had overheard, her salvation was so small, so ineffective, that it was beaten . . . by a brownie. Not by atheism or the edge of a sword, but by a baked good. *What exactly,* I asked myself, *was she saved from? What was I saved from?*

At that time, I was a teenager still struggling with very teenage problems. If this is what salvation meant for *her*, the best example I had, what hope was there for me?

I stood there, questioning what I believed.

The creator of heaven and earth became man, died a gruesome death, conquered the grave, lives inside of us—and what is the result? We're beaten by brownies. Or the internet. Or rush hour traffic. The slightest difficulty or temptation topples us like a house of cards. Why even call that "salvation?" What are Christians saved from?

I couldn't think of anything. At least, not anything in everyday life.

It may sound like an overreaction, and it was. There were plenty of Christians all around me living like Christ. But as I look back almost two decades later, it is these unanswered questions, these tiny inconsistencies, these moments of dissonance and doubt, that shipwreck lives. If salvation doesn't work in crisis—when we're tempted, fragile, or alone—it might as well not work at all. When hurting people come to the church looking for answers and we come back with technicalities, exceptions, and reasons why it won't work, they give up and start looking elsewhere. I couldn't articulate any of what I was feeling at the time and neither can many backslidden Christians. But I was longing for something more than forgiveness. I wanted incarnation. I needed the power of God to dwell in and empower my flesh.

Years later, I found what I was looking for in the Nicene Creed, "Who for us men and for our *salvation* came down from heaven and was *incarnate*."

Salvation and incarnation, spirit and flesh, go together. The reason I, and so many Christians I knew, were beaten by our various "brownies" was that we tried to have one without the other. We believed in salvation but not incarnation, and the result was frustration. Flesh wasn't the problem—it was the gospel we preached.

THE GOSPEL OF PLATO

Athanasius the Great was in his late twenties when he attended the Council of Nicaea—only he wasn't called "great" at the time. He was still a deacon, serving as a secretary to the patriarch of Alexandria, but was one of the intellectual giants of the Council. He went on to write *On the Incarnation*, one of the all-time classics on the subject. In this book, Athanasius compared God "becoming man" to an artist restoring a faded masterpiece,

> When a portrait painted on a panel has disappeared in consequence of external stains, there is need again for him to come whose the portrait is, that the likeness may be renewed on the same material; because for the sake of his picture the material itself on which it has been painted is not thrown away, but the likeness is retraced upon it: so, similarly, the All-holy Son of the Father, being the Image of the Father, came into our sphere to renew man made after Himself, and to find him as one lost.[83]

You are made in the image of God,[84] and not just your spirit or your soul. Your body is the physical material on which God's image is traced—the canvas he fashioned for his self-portrait. Sin and self-righteousness can stain and obscure the image until it is no longer recognizable, but the image is still there, latent within and in need of restoration. For this reason, Jesus came down from heaven. "The Son of Man has come to seek and to save that which is lost" (Luke 19:10, NKJV). To *seek* and to *save*—not to throw away and start over.

Read the seventh chapter of Romans, however, and it is possible to come away with a very different view of grace, salvation, and the human condition—one where there is nothing about us worth saving, particularly in our bodies,

> For I know that nothing good dwells in me, that is, in my flesh. For I have the desire to do what is right, but not the ability to carry it out. (Romans 7:18)

> Now if I do what I do not want, it is no longer I who do it, but sin that dwells within me. (Romans 7:20)

> Wretched man that I am! Who will deliver me from this body of death? (Romans 7:24)

These are challenging verses, but somewhere between Athanasius' day and today, we started reading them differently. The modern understanding of Romans 7 goes like this: As Christians, we want to do what is right but can't because our bodies get in the way. Fortunately, there is grace so at least we're not responsible when we, or rather "our flesh," fall into sin. Growing in virtue means not feeling condemned no matter what we do. We're not the ones doing wrong—it is sin within us.

Athanasius wouldn't recognize this as Christianity. Neither would Paul. For the ancient church, Christianity meant being like Christ. They knew their bodies were made in God's image and chose to share in the life of their savior with every fiber of their being. They longed to imitate Christ. Even to suffer and to die with Christ. Their faith was a physical, hands-on experience. The idea that spirit is good and flesh is bad is the gospel of Plato—not the gospel of Paul.

Scripture bestows the highest possible dignity on the flesh: *God became it*. The flesh, and our sometimes-tumultuous relationship with it, can be understood only in light of this fact. What, then, are we to make of such strong, and seemingly contradictory, statements in Romans 7, "Who will deliver me from this body of death?" (v. 24) and "Nothing good dwells in me, that is, in my flesh" (v. 18)?

UNITED AGAIN

In his book, *Biblical Ethics*, Oswald Chambers worked through the difficult passages in Romans 7 the same way the early church did—by keeping his eyes fixed on the Incarnation. He began by explaining Paul's context,

> The 7th of Romans represents the profound conflict which goes on in the consciousness of a man without the Spirit of God, facing the demands of God.... It is the presentation by a man who stands now as a saint, looking back on the terrific conflict produced by his conscience having been awakened to the law of God, but with no power to do what his mind assigns he should.[85]

In this chapter, Paul is describing the angst of "a man without the Spirit of God"—an unbeliever facing the demands of salvation without the grace of incarnation. Such a person knows that "nothing good dwells in me, that is, in my flesh" (Romans 7:18) and so cries out in desperation, "Who will deliver me from this body of death?" (Romans 7:24).

Why would a Christian say such things? We believe that salvation and incarnation go together. We believe that the greatest good, God himself, dwells within us. That is, in our flesh. "Do you not know that Jesus Christ is in you?" (2 Corinthians 13:5). "Do you not know that *your body* is a temple of the Holy Spirit within you, whom you have from God?" (1 Corinthians 6:19, emphasis added).

For those who don't know these powerful truths, life is as Paul described in Romans 7. A struggle. A war between the love of God and the lust of the flesh. Oswald Chambers could barely stand the thought,

> If all God can do for me is to destroy the unity I once had, make me a divided personality, give me light that makes me morally insane with longing to do what I cannot do, I would rather be without His salvation, rather remain happy and peaceful without Him.[86]

These are strong words, but the honesty is refreshing. Who hasn't questioned their salvation? Or had second thoughts when faith didn't turn out to be a walk in the park?

Don't sweep such feelings under the rug. Be honest with yourself. If you're beaten by brownies or anything else, dare to ask why. Doing so is the first step toward breaking the habit and experiencing true freedom. Oswald Chambers let the spirit/flesh dilemma guide him into an abiding hope in the Incarnation. He continued,

> But if this experience is only a stage towards a life of union with God, it is a different matter.[87]

The Incarnation is, simply, "a life of union with God." For this reason, the prophets called Jesus *Immanuel*—"God with us."[88] How is God with us? In every way. Spiritually, mentally, even physically. "Glorify and bear about God in your body,"[89] Cyprian of Carthage wrote, quoting the Latin version of 1 Corinthians 6:20. Consider the magnitude of this statement. You carry God with you. His real presence is wherever you are.

Jesus was the Word made flesh, but if you "glorify and bear about God in your body," then *you* make his words flesh to everyone you meet. You show God through your hands when you work hard, help those less fortunate, and build up others instead of tearing them down. You show God through your feet when you walk humbly, go the distance, and stand unwavering in your convictions. You show God through your whole self when you embrace those others won't; when you refuse to let your eyes wander and instead hunger and thirst after the right things; when you willingly give of yourself without hope of or desire for repayment.

But what if your actions don't honor him? Is God still with you and in you? The answer is sobering.

Earlier in the same chapter of 1 Corinthians, Paul wrote, "Do you not know that your bodies are members of Christ? Shall I then take the members of Christ and make them members of a prostitute? Never!" (1 Corinthians 6:15). As a Christian, God's real presence is wherever you are—no matter what you are doing. This is why sin is so tragic. Before you act, ask yourself, *Will what I am about to do represent God as he truly is—as his image in the world—or will it hide, disgrace, or distort him?*

Leo the Great encouraged us always to choose the former, "Christian, acknowledge thy dignity, and becoming a partner in the Divine nature, refuse to return to the old baseness by degenerate conduct."[90]

Becoming a partner in or "partaker of the divine nature" (2 Peter 1:4) implies that there are two natures inside of you—one human, the other divine. Where does one nature stop and the other begin? Similar questions were asked of Jesus. Which nature walked on water? Healed the sick? Died on the cross? Rose from the dead? The truth of the Incarnation is that a nature didn't do any of these things. An individual did—a *person* named Jesus Christ in whom God and man worked together instead of tearing each other apart. When you make the right decision or the wrong one, when you live up to what you believe or fall short, a nature isn't responsible. It's not your spirit or your flesh. It's you—a *person* in whom God and man can work together. The choice is yours.

"The gospel faith proclaims the union of God and man,"[91] Hilary of Poitiers wrote, but it also proclaims union within our hearts. With ourselves. "Unite my heart to fear your name," (Psalm 86:11) David prayed. And Paul said, "Now may the God of peace himself *sanctify you completely*, and may your *whole* spirit and soul and body be kept blameless at the coming of our Lord Jesus Christ" (1 Thessalonians 5:23, emphasis added). Instead of the "divided personality" Oswald Chambers warned of, begin to see yourself in this light. United. Able to "love the Lord your God with all your heart and with all your soul and with all your strength and with all your mind" (Luke 10:27). In the Incarnation, no part of you is left out. "He in His entirety assumed me in my entirety... so that he might bestow grace upon the whole,"[92] John of Damascus wrote. "Let us become like Christ," Gregory Nazianzus said, "since Christ became like us."[93]

MADE FOR THIS

After affirming that Jesus "came down from heaven and was incarnate," the Creed states that he "became man." This may seem like another way of saying the same thing, but it's not. Being human is more than looking like one. Apes bear a passing resemblance and share 98.8 percent of our DNA,[94] but they're not us.

Jesus was.

In order to fully appreciate the Incarnation, we need to know what being human means in more than just a biological sense. The book of Genesis recounts how God said, "Let us make man in our image, after our likeness" (Genesis 1:26) and then he "formed the [first] man of dust from the ground and breathed into his nostrils the breath of life, and the man became a living creature" (Genesis 2:7). From the beginning, you were made for communion with God. Being human meant physical union with God—"clay which was even then putting on the image of Christ,"[95] in the words of Tertullian.

Note that Tertullian said we were created in "the image of Christ" and not "the image of God." Why? For the earliest Christians, being made in God's image meant being made like Christ who is the one, true "image of the invisible God" (Colossians 1:15). To be human was and is to be like Christ and he "only did what he saw the Father doing" (John 5:19). There is dignity in humanity. We were made to be "like our teacher" (Luke 6:40).

An ancient mosaic in the cathedral of Monreale beautifully illustrates this principle. The story in the mosaic is a familiar one: Adam and Eve have just eaten the forbidden fruit and are about to be banished from paradise by Jesus himself. What is shocking in this image is the similarity between Adam and Christ. Apart from their expressions, they look identical. Even in a fallen state, Adam is clearly made like Christ—but he massively failed to live up to who he was. From then on, to be human was to fall short.

But you weren't made for failure. You were made for deep and abiding communion with God—for walking with him "in the cool of the day"

(Genesis 3:8) and not merely returning to the dust "out of [which] you were taken" (Genesis 3:19). The Incarnation reminded us whose image we were created in. We saw "the glory of God in the face of Jesus Christ" (2 Corinthians 4:6) and, step by step, began to be "transformed into the same image from one degree of glory to another" (2 Corinthians 3:18). We couldn't do it on our own. We needed an Incarnate God. Someone to hold our hand and pick us up when we fall. Athanasius said it this way,

> For as a good teacher who is concerned for his pupils, when they are unable to be benefited by the more difficult subjects, condescends to them, and teaches at least by easier methods; so also did the Word of God.[96]

In other words, God came down to our level, to lift us up to his, so that we could be as he always intended.

With him.

Are you with him? Do you do the things Christians do so you can look down on those who don't and feel better about yourself? Or do you pray, go to church, read the Bible, follow the commandments, and give of yourself and your time simply because you want to be with him? Either way, your actions will be the same, but there is a world of difference between the two. Going through the motions will fail to satisfy. Being with him is what you were made for. It is where you will find fulfillment, purpose, and peace. "Come to me, all you who labor and are heavy laden," Jesus said, "and you will find rest for your souls" (Matthew 11:28-29). You will find your soul. You will find yourself in the Incarnation.

God became man. But even though he could have, he didn't do it on his own.

Next the Nicene Creed indicates how the Incarnation took place. The Son of God "was incarnate of the Holy Spirit *and* the Virgin Mary."

*"Obtain through grace

what you have not

by nature."*

—LEO THE GREAT

9

BORN OF A VIRGIN

*"My little children, for whom I am again in the anguish
of childbirth until Christ is formed in you!"*
(Galatians 4:19)

AND.

One syllable. Three letters. The kind of word we skim over without much thought.

But sometimes "and" can make all the difference in the world. It does in the Nicene Creed.

In the previous chapter, we explored the effects of the Incarnation—what God becoming flesh means for our flesh. In doing so, we took the Incarnation at face value without delving into the historical events that made it possible. How did God become one of us? According to the Nicene Creed, he was "incarnate of the Holy Spirit and the Virgin Mary." The Incarnation wasn't something God did while everyone else sat back and watched. For God to become man, both God and man—or more specifically, a young woman—had important roles to play.

The Spirit *and* Mary.

It has been said that "we contribute nothing to our salvation except the sin that made it necessary." Of course, we can't earn our way to heaven as we saw in Chapter Seven. But "contributing nothing" goes to the opposite extreme and bypasses the virgin birth; not just the historical reality, but also the underlying principle that "God, the all-sufficient, depended upon" someone "in order to effect our salvation."[97] Salvation wouldn't be possible without a contribution from one of our own—a young woman, in and through whom the Word became flesh.

There are so many opinions on Mary. Some Christians idolize her; others barely acknowledge she existed. But instead of wading into that debate, let's focus on how the Incarnation took place. How did a virgin become a mother—"the mother of our Lord" (Luke 1:43), no less? The answer is in the first chapter of Luke's gospel,

> In the sixth month the angel Gabriel was sent from God to a city of Galilee named Nazareth, to a virgin betrothed to a man whose name was Joseph, of the house of David. And the virgin's name was Mary. And he came to her and said, "Greetings, O *favored one*, the Lord is with you!" (Luke 1:26-28, emphasis added)

Here "favored one" means someone "endowed with grace"[98] according to A.T. Robertson's *Word Pictures in the New Testament*. And that is how Gabriel's greeting to Mary was traditionally understood. Instead of "favored one," some English versions of the New Testament,[99] and many of the church fathers[100] use the expression "full of grace." Ambrose of Milan provides a classic example in his *Three Books on the Holy Spirit*,

> Gabriel himself, when sent to Mary, said: "Hail, full of grace," plainly declaring the grace of the Spirit which was in her, because the Holy Spirit had come upon her, she was about to have her womb full of grace with the heavenly Word.[101]

Note what Ambrose said Mary used grace to do. To "continue in sin that grace may abound" (Romans 6:1)? No. "She was about to have her womb full of grace with the heavenly Word." That is, *Mary used grace to make the Word flesh.*

> Do not be afraid, Mary, for you have found favor [grace] with God. And behold, you will conceive in your womb and bear a son, and you shall call his name Jesus. (Luke 1:30-31)

The Virgin Mary and grace—two lightning rod topics, both of which are the subject of this chapter. Some of what lies ahead may be challenging. It may bring back memories of the tradition you were raised in, where God felt a million miles away. Or it may contradict what you've heard on the same subjects from today's most popular Christian authors and speakers. Controversy aside, it would be easy to skip over this phrase of the Creed for another reason—it wasn't in the original. "Of the Holy Spirit and the Virgin Mary" is an addition made at the Council of Constantinople in the year 381. Faithful Christians recited the Creed for fifty-six years without one word about Mary.

But something was missing. Without this phrase, it was possible to think of salvation in an ahistorical way, that is, in a way that ignores what really happened. God could have become man on his own, the way he created everything out of nothing, but he didn't. Likewise, he could make us develop in his character without our involvement, but he won't. Christianity requires the Holy Spirit and you. There is an "and" there—a synergy between you and God called grace. Grace is not automatic, as much as we may want it to be. Instead, Peter encouraged us to "grow in the grace and knowledge of . . . Jesus Christ" (2 Peter 3:18) day by day.

For centuries, Christians did just that by focusing on a particular chapter of the life of Christ—his birth.

WAR ON CHRISTMAS

Of all the events in the New Testament, few have sparked more debate than the virgin birth.

It wasn't that a woman was pregnant out of wedlock. That was old news even in the first century. It wasn't that a virgin gave birth. The prophet Isaiah foretold this miracle centuries before it occurred.[102] It was who was born. Augustine summarized the controversy in a single sentence, "Realize that it was God who was born, and you will not be surprised at a virgin giving birth."[103]

God, by definition, is eternal. The scriptures call him "the Ancient of Days" (Daniel 7:9) and the "One who inhabits eternity" (Isaiah 57:15, NKJV). Imagine the shock then when the shepherds heard the angelic announcement of Jesus' birth, "For unto you is born this day in the city of David a Savior, who is Christ the Lord" (Luke 2:11). Or what the church in Galatia must have thought after reading Paul's words, "God sent forth his Son, born of woman, born under the law" (Galatians 4:4). God cannot be born—and yet he was.

Today, most of us are either okay with or unaware of this paradox. Our biggest "theological" concern at Christmas is avoiding the phrase "happy holidays." In the fourth and fifth centuries, however, there was a real war on, or at least over, Christmas. The debate was about Jesus—who he was at the time of his conception and birth—but oddly enough, the battle lines were drawn over what to call Mary.

In Luke 1:43, Mary's relative Elizabeth addressed her as "the mother of my Lord." What does "Lord" mean in this context? Since God being born is such a hard pill to swallow, some tried to explain away the controversy by saying Mary was the mother of the human part of Jesus or the baby who would grow up to become the Son of God. But the majority understood "Lord" to mean what it does in the rest of scripture—God. *From miraculous conception to virgin birth, there was no time that the child Mary carried within her was not fully God and fully man.*

Think what this means. Paul wrote that in the person of Jesus Christ "the whole fullness of deity dwells bodily" (Colossians 2:9). By carrying her baby to term, "the whole fullness of deity dwelled bodily" in Mary. At least—it did for nine months.

One of the greatest miracles of the virgin birth is that Mary lived to talk about it.

The book of Exodus records how Moses built a gilded chest to contain the Ten Commandments. This chest was known as the Ark of the Covenant and was the point of contact between God and his people. "There I will meet with you," (Exodus 25:22) God promised Moses. The Ark came to embody God's presence on earth—a presence so holy that, on more than one occasion, people died from touching the same material God did.[104] "Our God is a consuming fire" (Hebrews 12:29). Why, then, wasn't Mary consumed? If the "heaven and the highest heaven cannot contain [God]" (1 Kings 8:27), how could a teenager from Nazareth?

Did God turn down his holiness so Mary could tolerate his presence? No, the scriptures are clear on this point. "I the Lord do not change" (Malachi 3:6). "Jesus Christ is the same yesterday and today and forever" (Hebrews 13:8). Leo the Great described the Incarnation as God "remaining what He was" while "assuming what He was not."[105] It wasn't God who changed in the virgin birth; it was Mary. The priests of old found grace to come "near to [God] himself" (Numbers 16:9) and minister in his temple. Mary found grace to contain God himself and for her body to become "the temple of the Holy Spirit" (1 Corinthians 6:19). In the words of the angel,

> The Holy Spirit will come upon you, and the power of the Most High will overshadow you; therefore the child to be born will be called holy—the Son of God. (Luke 1:35)

God's power "came upon" and "overshadowed" Mary. But Mary had something of her own to contribute to the Incarnation. Herself. She said, "Let it be to me according to your word" (Luke 1:38)—the biblical equivalent of "yes"—and then embraced all the shame, uncertainty, rejection, and morning sickness that went along with her answer.

The Word became flesh, but only because Mary cooperated with grace.

Whatever you've heard about grace—whether it is unmerited, prevenient, costly, revolutionary, or just plain amazing—the point is to do more than receive it. Participate in it until it has the same effect in your life as it did in Mary's. Until Christ is formed in you. Paul wrote to the Galatians,

> My little children, for whom I am again in the anguish of childbirth *until Christ is formed in you!* (Galatians 4:19, emphasis added)

What does this mean? How is Christ formed in us? He became flesh over two thousand years ago. Jesus has already been born and doesn't need to be born again.

But we do.

REBORN

"You must be born again."

So said Jesus to a religious leader named Nicodemus and to us by extension. When Nicodemus didn't understand how someone could "enter a second time into his mother's womb and be born" (John 3:4), Jesus clarified,

> That which is born of the flesh is flesh, and that which is born of the Spirit is spirit. Do not marvel that I said to you, "You must be born again." (John 3:6–7)

Today, "born again" is a loaded term. It carries social, political, and religious connotations; so much so that "born-again Christian" is a demographic group studied by pollsters. Nicodemus had no such context. All he knew was that Jesus compared spiritual formation to natural birth.

As I write this, my wife is pregnant with our first child and birth is on both our minds. Anyone who has taken a high school health class knows that there is a gestation period of nine months from conception to birth. But you begin to appreciate just how much of a process this is when you go through it—or help someone else go through it.

Every day my wife checks an app on her phone that tells her about the new life developing inside—how the baby has grown, what she should expect to feel, and steps for a successful pregnancy. The first time she opened the app, there was an illustration of the baby that looked nothing like us. But as the weeks went by, that little bundle of cells began to take shape. We can see more and more of ourselves day by day. There are two eyes—whose color will they be? A little heart—beating with our blood. Tiny hands—that we can't wait to hold in ours.

Nicodemus lived in a day before smartphones and ultrasound, but similar thoughts must have gone through his mind. Spiritual birth takes time. It is a process of growing up into God's image.

Many of us can look back to a specific moment where our walk of faith began. Like Mary, we said "yes" to God and our lives changed. The transformation was real, but is a one-time decision what Jesus had in mind when he said, "You must be born again" (John 3:7)? Birth without an adequate period of formation is called miscarriage and, sadly, that is the outcome of far too many conversion stories. How many Christians do you know who started strong then fell away? Or who "come to the altar" at every opportunity because they are never fully convinced of their salvation?

When Paul wrote to the Galatians "I am in the anguish of childbirth until Christ is formed in you" (Galatians 4:19), he was talking about spiritual formation—the process whereby we "grow up in every way into [Christ]" (Ephesians 4:15). This doesn't happen in an instant. It's not glamorous or showy. In fact, spiritual formation starts with something so small you may not detect it. Peter called it a seed. "You have been born again, not of perishable seed but of imperishable, through the living and abiding word of God" (1 Peter 1:23). So did John, "No one born of God makes a practice of sinning, for God's seed abides in him; and he cannot keep on sinning, because he has been born of God" (1 John 3:9).

Breaking sinful habits is only the start of the Christian life. Now the real transformation can begin. It takes time and can be uncomfortable. Sometimes we look nothing like what we will become. There may be days where we wake up and are sick of it all. But if we stay the course, Christ will be formed in us. Our nature will change. We will begin to "love righteousness" (Psalm 45:7) rather than merely abstaining from what is wrong. Instead of lashing out, our first reaction will be to "bless those who curse us" and "pray for those who abuse us" (Luke 6:28)—even on the freeway. Our honest desire will be to "refuse the evil and choose the good" (Isaiah 7:16). "A Christian," John Climacus wrote, "is an imitator of Christ in thought, word and deed, as far as this is humanly possible."[106] And how far is possible? Jesus removed all limits, "You therefore must be perfect, as your heavenly Father is perfect" (Matthew 5:48).

To be "born again" is what it sounds like—to be re-born to an entirely different way of life. Augustine said it this way,

> We shall be made truly free, then, when God fashions us, that is, forms and creates us anew, not as men—for He has done that already—but as good men, which His grace is now doing, that we may be a new creation in Christ Jesus.[107]

None of us is good by nature. "No one is good except God alone" (Luke 18:19). But, in the words of Leo the Great, we can "obtain through grace" what we did not have "by nature."[108] Grace transforms us into what we could not otherwise be. Jesus is the only begotten Son of God. There is no other. And yet we have "the right to become children of God" (John 1:12) by adoption. Christ by nature, us by grace—all participating in the same divine life. "We shall be like him" (1 John 3:2). This is the gospel of grace.

But as amazing as grace is, there is one thing it never can be—a solo activity. Jesus "was incarnate of the Holy Spirit *and* the Virgin Mary." That conjunction means that if you want to grow in grace, you have to participate.

Effort is involved.

GROWING IN GRACE

In an essay entitled *Live Life to the Full*, Dallas Willard, professor of philosophy at the University of Southern California, briefly summarized how to grow in grace,

"Grace is not opposed to effort. It is opposed to earning."[109]

Like anything worth having, grace requires effort on our part. It is how the Word became flesh.

In the virgin birth, Mary received grace. The Holy Spirit came upon her and the power of the Most High overshadowed her.[110] John Chrysostom marveled at this in his famous Nativity sermon, "Nature here rested, while the Will of God labored. O ineffable grace!"[111] But after receiving so much grace that the church fathers called her "full," Mary still had to carry a baby for nine months. As any mother knows, pregnancy requires effort. And while church tradition varies on the more intimate details of Jesus' birth, pregnancies typically end with even more effort. It is called "labor" for a reason—especially in a time before modern medicine. Labor, discomfort, even pain: these are not words that we typically associate with grace.

But Paul did.

> But by the grace of God I am what I am, and His grace toward me was not in vain; but I labored more abundantly than they all, yet not I, but the grace of God which was with me. (1 Corinthians 15:10)

> So to keep me from becoming conceited because of the surpassing greatness of the revelations, a thorn was given me in the flesh, a messenger of Satan to harass me, to keep me from becoming conceited. Three times I pleaded with the Lord about this, that it should leave me. But he said to me, *"My grace is sufficient for you,* for my power is made perfect in weakness." Therefore I will boast all the more gladly of my weaknesses, so that the power of Christ may rest upon me. For the sake of Christ, then, I am content with weaknesses, insults, hardships, persecutions, and calamities. For when I am weak, then I am strong. (2 Corinthians 12:7-10, emphasis added)

There isn't a hint of earning in verses like these. But there is a great deal of effort. "Everyone to whom much was given, of him much will be required" (Luke 12:48). God expects us to do something with the grace he gives us and for it to have a meaningful, tangible effect in our lives, just as it did for Mary and for Paul.

Sometimes the line is thin between earning grace and effort because of grace. Think of the person who wakes up early to study the Bible and pray, not to learn about God and spend time in his presence, but as a sort of good luck charm or way to keep God happy. How many donate to charity, go on missions trips, or volunteer at soup kitchens out of a sense of necessity or obligation, rather than from genuine compassion? There are times we need to do things that we don't want to, but where are our hearts in such moments? Why do we do what we do?

"Grace is not opposed to effort. It is opposed to earning." Think of it like a dance: God leads, we follow. And the sometimes-painful process of growing in grace is learning to dance. Sometimes we get ahead of God. Other times we fall behind. Occasionally we step on his feet. We stumble. But we get up again and keep going, growing closer to our Savior with every step.

At any given moment, we are being asked to dance—to say "yes" or "no" to grace. What must have gone through Mary's mind when she answered the angel? The punishment for adultery in Israel at that time was death.[112] She didn't know if Joseph would take her back. And yet, despite every reason to the contrary, Mary said, "Yes, I'll dance." Then, and only then, did the Word become flesh. What about you? You may have every right to hate the person who wronged you, but will you dance anyway and find the strength to walk in forgiveness? Maybe you have struggled with a particular vice for years, and every time you stumble, you let go of God. But instead of being self-conscious and leaving the dancefloor in shame, will you dance anyway until you have mastered the steps to overcome temptation?

There is nothing wrong with learning to dance. In fact, learning is the only way to dance well. In the same essay, Dallas Willard spoke of developing the discipline to grow in grace, or any other skill. "A discipline in any area is something in my power that I do to enable me to do what I cannot do by direct effort."[113] No one is born knowing multiple languages, or any language for that matter. Few are under par the first time they play golf. Almost everything worthwhile in human experience is learned and mastered through discipline—by doing the same thing over and over and over again until it becomes second nature. Dallas Willard continued,

> Disciplines are for disciples—apprentices—of Jesus, not for dabblers or mere consumers of religious services. They are for people who intend to learn from Jesus how to live their whole lives in the kingdom of God as he would live their lives if he were they.[114]

Traditionally, the church is the place where these spiritual disciplines were mastered. Through the recitation of the Creed, reading of scripture, singing of the Psalms, participation in the sacraments, regimented fasting, and contemplative prayer, ancient Christians learned how to grow in grace. We may look back at these earlier times and look down on the amount of effort put into living the Christian life. *If only they understood grace*, we might think to ourselves.

But perhaps the reason the ancient church did so much with so little is that they *did* understand grace. Maybe we are the ones who need to learn how to dance. And we can—if we allow those who already perfected the art of Christian living to show us the steps.

> But grow in the grace and knowledge of our Lord and Savior Jesus Christ. To him be the glory both now and to the day of eternity. Amen. (2 Peter 3:18)

After Jesus' birth, the Nicene Creed fast-forwards thirty-three years to his death, but the subject is still the Incarnation. How far did it go? How far *can* it go? When God became man, he didn't just take on the good parts; he embraced everything that being human means, including suffering, pain, and even death.

In the Incarnation, God died.

"*Permit me

to be an imitator

of the passion

of my God.*"

—IGNATIUS OF ANTIOCH

10

CRUCIFIED FOR US

*"That I may know him and the power of his resurrection,
and may share his sufferings, becoming like him in his death."*
(Philippians 3:10)

It was late June 1939—less than forty-five days before the start of the Second World War—and Dietrich Bonhoeffer decided to return to Nazi Germany. As a leader of the German underground church, Bonhoeffer opposed Adolf Hitler's rise to power. He had fled to America to avoid serving in a military force bent on subjecting Europe to authoritarian rule, but after less than a month in the United States, Bonhoeffer was on a ship bound for his troubled homeland. He wrote to an old friend,

> I have made a mistake in coming to America. I must live through this difficult period of our national history with the Christian people of Germany. I will have no right to participate in the reconstruction of Christian life in Germany after the war if I do not share the trials of this time with my people.[115]

On April 9, 1945—six years after his return and only thirty days before the end of the war in Europe—Dietrich Bonhoeffer was executed at the

Flossenbürg concentration camp. "He was one of the most capable and brave theologians of the Confessing Church," a friend wrote upon hearing of his death. "He has entered church history as one of those martyrs of whom it is written, 'If we have died with him, we will also live with him; if we endure, we will also reign with him!'"[116]

Why did Bonhoeffer go back? In America, he could write and publish freely. He would do more good alive than dead. There were other pastors, other Christians, in Germany. It wasn't his war to fight.

And yet, Bonhoeffer returned. He suffered and died with his people. For him, being a member of the "body of Christ" included suffering with Christ. He said it like this in his classic book, first published in English under the title *The Cost of Discipleship*,

> The bond between Jesus and the disciples who followed him was a bodily bond. This was no accident but a necessary consequence of the incarnation. A prophet and teacher would not need followers, but only students and listeners. But the incarnate Son of God who took on human flesh does need a community of followers . . . who not only participate in his teaching but also in his body.[117]

For Bonhoeffer, the Incarnation was more than the virgin birth. It included everything Jesus grew up to do, say, and even suffer. The Nicene Creed takes a similar approach. It states that God "became man" then focuses on the one event that illustrates just how human he became.

His death.

> [We believe] in one Lord, Jesus Christ . . . [who] was crucified for us under Pontius Pilate, and suffered, and was buried.

God being born was one thing. But how do you "crucify the Lord of glory" (1 Corinthians 2:8) or "kill the Author of life" (Acts 3:15)? God doesn't suffer. He cannot die. And yet, the scriptures state that Jesus—"true

God and eternal life" (1 John 5:20)—was "a man of sorrows . . . acquainted with grief" (Isaiah 53:3). He learned "obedience through what he suffered" (Hebrews 5:8) and "humbled himself . . . to the point of death, even death on a cross" (Philippians 2:8). Are these metaphors? Did Jesus only appear to suffer and die? Bonhoeffer didn't think so. Neither did the ancient church. They believed, despite the apparent contradiction, that "one of the Trinity suffered in the flesh."[118] This belief empowered them to face their own paradoxes—embracing suffering rather than running from it and living lives that challenge us to this day.

When we, as modern Christians, read that Jesus was "crucified for us" we tend to miss the controversy of who was crucified and go straight to the part about us. Jesus died *for us*, satisfying the demands of justice *for our* sins. But atonement is only part of the picture. It can't explain why Bonhoeffer returned to Nazi Germany, make sense of a miscarriage, give a community hope after a mass shooting, or even account for much of the New Testament.

> Christ also suffered for you, leaving you an example, so *that you might follow in his steps*. (1 Peter 2:21, emphasis added)

> Now I rejoice in my sufferings for your sake, and *in my flesh I am filling up what is lacking in Christ's afflictions* for the sake of his body, that is, the church. (Colossians 1:24, emphasis added)

> That I may know him and the power of his resurrection, and may *share his sufferings, becoming like him in his death*, that by any means possible I may attain the resurrection from the dead. (Philippians 3:10-11, emphasis added)

These scriptures are about Christ's death, but have little, if anything, to do with atonement. There is another dimension to the cross—one that, in the words of Bonhoeffer, requires "not only participating in his teaching but also in his body."[119]

IMITATING THE PASSION

From the perspective of the Incarnation, and the depth of devotion it traditionally inspired, the cross looks very different. It is something God did as one of us and is another opportunity for us to be like him.

"Be imitators of God," Paul wrote. How? By "walking in love, as Christ loved us and gave himself up for us, a fragrant offering and sacrifice to God" (Ephesians 5:1-2). *Christianity means imitating Christ—in his death, as well as in his life.*

Many throughout history took this literally.

"Permit me to be an imitator of the passion of my God,"[120] Ignatius of Antioch wrote while on the way to Rome in the early second century. Ignatius was a prisoner for his faith and knew that martyrdom awaited him in the capital, but he wasn't afraid to die for Christ. He feared that, out of their love for him, the Christians in Rome would pray or exert political pressure to release him—thereby depriving him of the greatest chance to be like his Lord.

"Now I begin to be a disciple,"[121] he remarked at the end of his life. Ignatius was seventy-three and had been a Christian from the time he was a boy. He was the bishop of the city where Christians were first called "Christians."[122] He received the faith from John—the "disciple whom Jesus loved" (John 21:20). But none of this mattered. Ignatius insisted that he could not "attain to Christ"[123] until he had made Christ's passion his own.

Imitating the passion isn't just for martyrs. It may look different for us than it did for Ignatius, but the New Testament encourages each of us to be *"crucified* with Christ" (Galatians 2:20), to *"suffer* with him" (Romans 8:17), and even to be *"buried* with him" (Colossians 2:12).

The three verbs the Nicene Creed uses to describe Jesus' death should characterize all our lives.

In the coming pages, we will experience Christ's passion for ourselves. No belief makes death an easy subject. Suffering will always hurt. But in the middle of hard times and difficult questions, the Incarnation will become for us what it was for men like Bonhoeffer and Ignatius—the power to *be*, and not just call ourselves, Christians.

CRUCIFIED WITH CHRIST

In a chapter about the cross, it is worth repeating that the Incarnation is not about death. It's about life. But dying is a fact of life, so the Incarnation must deal with it. A pastor and popular author described the opposing forces in the Incarnation like this, "God entered the world in order to take on the fullness of human existence, which means not only the fullness of human life, but also the fullness of human death."[124]

In experiencing "the fullness of human death," Jesus didn't die as a great man or a hero. He was, in the words of the Nicene Creed, "crucified for us."

Today, we hear the term "crucifixion" and think Christianity. There was no such association in the first century. The *crux* was the lowest of the low—a worse form of punishment than being burnt alive, beheaded, or torn apart by wild animals in the arena.[125] Jesus died as a slave, and his followers were accused of worshipping "a criminal and his cross."[126] The first Christians had to deal with the fact that not only did their God die, but he also died the most shameful of deaths.

The cross was too much for many would-be Christians. Some denied it altogether. The Incarnation couldn't go *that* far. Others went to the opposite extreme and said that if Jesus died on the cross, he couldn't have been God. He was less than the Father—a little "g" god who could suffer and die. This was the argument of Arius and refuting it was one of the goals of the Council of Nicaea.

But try as they might, no one could explain away the scandal. God can't die. Good men aren't crucified. Jesus was both and did both. On the cross, he challenged every assumption of how divinity and humanity should look. This had a profound effect on those who witnessed it. "Truly this man was the Son of God!" (Mark 15:39), marveled a soldier who was there. Paul expanded on the centurion's words in his letter to the Philippians,

> Let this mind be in you which was also in Christ Jesus, who, being in the form of God, did not consider it robbery to be equal with God, but made Himself of no reputation, taking the form of a bondservant, and coming in the likeness of men. And being found in appearance as a man, He humbled Himself and became obedient to the point of death, even the death of the cross. (Philippians 2:5–8, NKJV)

Many scholars believe verses six through eight are a song, possibly written in Aramaic, sung by one of the first Christian communities and quoted by Paul. It is among the most theologically dense sections of scripture, yet the meaning couldn't be simpler for those who sang it.

"Let this mind be in you. . ."

The pages of church history are filled with stories of men and women who laid down their lives for the faith. We have seen two of them already. But even more than dying for Christ, these Christians wanted to *live* for him—to possess the same mind, character, and love that they saw uncensored on the cross. This is one of the most repeated themes in the New Testament,

> Be imitators of God, as beloved children. And walk in love, as Christ loved us and gave himself up for us, a fragrant offering and sacrifice to God. (Ephesians 5:1-2)

> Since therefore Christ suffered in the flesh, arm yourselves with the same way of thinking, for whoever has suffered in the flesh has ceased from sin, so as to live for the rest of the time in the flesh no longer for human passions but for the will of God. (1 Peter 4:1–2)

> I have been crucified with Christ. It is no longer I who live, but Christ who lives in me. And the life I now live in the flesh I live by faith in the Son of God, who loved me and gave himself for me. (Galatians 2:20)

The first time I saw Mel Gibson's film *The Passion of the Christ*, it moved me to tears. Seeing what the crucifixion might have been like was hard enough. Enduring it, and doing so willingly, was beyond the realm of comprehension. I left the theater with a profound sense of gratitude that Jesus did so much for me—but thankfulness was all I felt. I never looked at Christ suffering on the big screen and dared to think that *I* could do the same or that *I* could love others in such a profound way.

But that is exactly how the ancient church saw it.

And that is why the Incarnation meant so much to them.

God became man—not superman. And in his humanity was everything necessary to live the life he lived and die the death he died. Those who saw him weren't just grateful for his sacrifice. They knew that they could follow in his steps—the very "footprints of the Lord's passion."[127] John of Damascus wrote,

> It was not as God alone that He freely delivered Himself over to death, but as man, also. Whence, He also gave us the grace of courage in the face of death. . . . setting for us a most noble example and pattern.[128]

THE WAY OF THE CROSS

How do we make the Incarnation the example and pattern for our lives? Jesus told us. "If anyone would come after me, let him deny himself and take up his cross and follow me. For whoever would save his life will lose it, but whoever loses his life for my sake and the gospel's will save it" (Mark 8:34-35).

The way of the cross ends with new life. It begins with self-denial. Denial means "esteeming others better than ourselves" (Philippians 2:3, NKJV), "not retaliating" (1 Peter 2:23, NLT) when we are insulted, "suffering wrong" (1 Corinthians 6:7) rather than proving ourselves right, and "despising the shame" (Hebrews 12:2) of being different. Only then can we take up the cross. Through self-control, we "crucify the flesh with its passions and desires" (Galatians 5:24), "put to death . . . what is earthly in us" (Colossians 3:5), and "die to sin" so that we can "live to righteousness" (1 Peter 2:24). Christ's passion frees us from our passions until "it is no longer we who live, but Christ who lives in us" (Galatians 2:20). We "always carry in the body the death of Jesus, so that the life of Jesus may also be manifested in our bodies" (2 Corinthians 4:10) knowing that "if we have died with him, we will also live with him; if we endure, we will also reign with him" (2 Timothy 2:11–12).

None of this is a one-time event. Luke's Gospel includes an important qualifier: "If anyone would come after me, let him deny himself and take up his cross *daily* and follow me" (Luke 9:23, emphasis added). We take up the cross and follow Christ not once at a defining moment in our lives, but each and every day until the way of the cross becomes our way of life. The nineteenth-century priest John Henry Newman said it like this,

> The self-denial which is the test of our faith must be daily. . . . The word *daily* implies, that the self-denial which is pleasing to Christ consists in little things. This is plain, for opportunity for great self-denials does not come every day. Thus to take up the cross of Christ is no great action done once for all, it consists in the continual practice of small duties which are distasteful to us.[129]

If we are unable or unwilling to be uncomfortable for Christ's sake—to forgo our rights, humble ourselves, and daily become like him in his death—then we remain "students and listeners."[130] We cannot call ourselves his followers. "Whoever does not bear his own cross and come after me cannot be my disciple" (Luke 14:27). It is impossible to "walk in the same way in which he walked" (1 John 2:6) apart from the cross. We will never know "the power of his resurrection" without first "becoming like him in his death" and "sharing in his sufferings" (Philippians 3:10).

THE GRACE TO SUFFER

Christ suffering on the cross has always been controversial, but the nature of the controversy has changed over time. Historically, the debate was *if* God could suffer. Today, a more common question is *why* he suffered. I once received a mass email from a major Christian publisher that summarized the way many modern Christians view Christ's passion in a single sentence, "Jesus died to free us from sickness, making suffering illegal."

In other words, "Jesus suffered so that we don't have to."

Such sentiments may comfort those who are hurting. Still, the vast majority of Christians in the history of the church would not recognize statements like these. How could they? Suffering was an everyday reality for many of them—they had the scars and empty seats at the dinner table to prove it. They also recited the scriptures daily in church, scriptures like these,

> We suffer with him in order that we may also be glorified with him. (Romans 8:17)

> It has been granted to you that for the sake of Christ you should not only believe in him but also suffer for his sake. (Philippians 1:29)

> If anyone suffers as a Christian, let him not be ashamed, but let him glorify God in that name. (1 Peter 4:16)

For the apostles who wrote these things and the men and women who desired to follow in their steps, Jesus didn't eliminate suffering. He transformed what it meant. In light of the Incarnation, the early church knew it was possible to suffer—not out of compulsion, human frailty, or weakness—but "as a Christian." And as with anything else we do as Christians, God "gives more grace" (James 4:6).

There is grace—even the grace to suffer.

Dietrich Bonhoeffer wrote of, and knew through experience, the "immeasurable grace to suffer 'for him.'"[131] Father Damien cared for a leper colony in Hawaii for over a decade before contracting the disease himself. Athanasius the Great was exiled on five separate occasions. But perhaps the most vivid example of the grace to suffer is Felicitas, a female slave who was martyred along with her mistress, Perpetua, in the early second century.

Felicitas was already many months pregnant when she, Perpetua, and several other Carthaginian Christians were imprisoned and sentenced to death for their faith. Roman law forbade the public execution of pregnant women, so as the appointed day neared and her due date was still far off, Felicitas feared she would be unable to die with her companions. They all prayed that the child would come early, their prayers were answered, and Felicitas gave birth to a healthy, albeit one month premature, baby girl. Three days later, Felicitas and Perpetua entered the arena and gave up their lives together.

Their story is sobering. But even more incredible is what Felicitas said as she gave birth. Tertullian, also from northern Africa and a contemporary of the events, recorded her words,

> Immediately after their prayer her pains came upon her, and when, with the difficulty natural to an eight months' delivery, in the labour of bringing forth she was sorrowing, some one of the servants of the *Cataractarii* [jailers] said to her, "You who are in such suffering now, what will you do when you are thrown to the beasts, which you despised when you refused to sacrifice?" And she replied, "Now it is I that suffer what I suffer; but then there will be another in me, who will suffer for me, because I also am about to suffer for Him." Thus

she brought forth a little girl, which a certain sister brought up as her daughter.[132]

Her powerful statement, "There will be another in me, who will suffer for me, because I also am about to suffer for Him" captures the essence of suffering as a Christian. It is not we who suffer—it is Christ in us. We don't have to find the strength.

Just the grace.

You may never need the grace to die for Christ as Felicitas did. But everyone who goes by the name "Christian" will need the grace to live for him. Sometimes living for Christ means "obtaining promises," "escaping the edge of the sword," "receiving back" loved ones from their deathbeds, and being "made strong out of weakness" (Hebrews 11:33-34). Other times, it means the opposite: being "mocked," "destitute," "afflicted," "mistreated," and "not receiving what is promised" (Hebrews 11:36-39). Grace isn't just for the good times—however much we may wish it to be. John Chrysostom said, "[Faith] both accomplishes great things and suffers great things."[133] And Paul wrote,

> I know how to be brought low, and I know how to abound. In any and every circumstance, I have learned the secret of facing plenty and hunger, abundance and need. I can do all things through Christ who strengthens me. (Philippians 4:12-13)

The point of the Incarnation is "God with us" (Matthew 1:23). It is impossible to appreciate how much God is with us if life always goes our way. But when things aren't easy, when tragedy strikes, when it looks like there is no way to make it—his presence becomes real for us. We step beyond ourselves and our frailties, weaknesses, and fears and discover that there truly is "another in us, who will suffer for us," enabling us to do and endure what is otherwise unimaginable.

In trying times, we know by experience that God is with us. We come to understand the incarnational reality of Christ on the cross.

Instead of being afraid of suffering, the first disciples "rejoiced that they were counted worthy to suffer dishonor for the name" of Christ (Acts 5:41). This isn't natural. It's supernatural. They willingly suffered and had joy in the middle of it because they knew that God was with them. What about you? If you are ridiculed for your beliefs, if someone has wronged you and doesn't deserve forgiveness, if you have lost a job or a loved one, will you look for the easiest way out? Or will you look inside to the Lord Jesus Christ who was crucified for you and find the strength to do what you could not do on your own? "I am bearing all this in order to suffer with him," Ignatius wrote, "while he, the perfect human being, empowers me."[134]

CONQUERING DEATH WITH HIM

Crucifixion victims were seldom buried. As a final act of humiliation, their bodies were left to hang indefinitely—serving as a warning for passers-by and as food for wild animals. Crucifixion was as dehumanizing a form of death as possible.

And yet, the Nicene Creed states that Jesus was both "crucified" and "buried." Such a claim would have raised eyebrows in the ancient world, especially given the emphasis the early church placed on both events. Paul said it was "of first importance" to believe that "Christ died for our sins in accordance with the Scriptures, that he was *buried*, [and] that he was raised on the third day" (1 Corinthians 15:3–4, emphasis added).

In the previous chapter, we saw that "the whole fullness of deity dwells bodily" (Colossians 2:9) in the person of Jesus Christ. Put another way, *Jesus was fully God and fully man from womb to tomb.* Mary contained the fullness of God himself for nine months. The tomb couldn't last three days. From the moment of Christ's death, the "graves were opened; and many bodies of the saints who had fallen asleep were raised" (Matthew 27:52, NKJV). Three days later, "God raised him up, loosing the pangs of death, because it was not possible for him to be held by it" (Acts 2:24).

The scandal of the cross is that God died. The scandal of the tomb is that a man conquered death. This is the theme of the sixteenth Psalm,

> Therefore my heart is glad, and my glory rejoices;
> My flesh also will rest in hope.
> For You will not leave my soul in Sheol,
> Nor will You allow Your Holy One to see corruption.
> You will show me the path of life;
> In Your presence is fullness of joy;
> At Your right hand are pleasures forevermore. (Psalm 16:9-11, NKJV)

Compare Psalm 16 with other scriptures about the grave. "In death there is no remembrance of [God]; in Sheol who will give you praise?" (Psalm 6:5). "Those who go down to the pit do not hope in your faithfulness" (Isaiah 28:18). "Is your steadfast love declared in the grave . . . ? Are your wonders known in the darkness?" (Psalm 88:11-12). "Shall the dead arise . . . ?" (Psalm 88:10, NKJV). The answer to all these questions is no—death is final. It means darkness, desolation, and separation from God.

At least, it did before Jesus died and was buried.

According to Peter,[135] Paul,[136] and many of the church fathers,[137] Psalm 16 is a description of Christ in the tomb. He did not experience corruption. Neither did his body decay. Instead, he rested in hope—the hope of resurrection.

Everyone who has been buried with him shares the same hope.

> Having been buried with him in baptism, in which you were
> also raised with him through faith in the powerful working of
> God, who raised him from the dead. And you, who were dead
> in your trespasses and the uncircumcision of your flesh, God
> made alive together with him. (Colossians 2:12-13)

> For if we have been united with him in a death like his, we shall certainly be united with him in a resurrection like his. (Romans 6:5)

As a Christian, death is different. It isn't sinking into darkness. It is closing your eyes. And when they open, Christ will be there—and all those who went before you. "He is not God of the dead, but of the living, for all live to him" (Luke 20:38). "Through his death he ... destroyed the one who has the power over death ... and delivered all those who through fear of death were subject to lifelong slavery" (Hebrews 2:14-15).

The earliest Christians were fearless. They believed the words of the gospel, that even if they were "put to death" for the name of Christ, "not a hair of their heads would perish" (Luke 21:16, 18). The grave wasn't final, so it wasn't fearful. They scorned death and the opponents of the cross who threatened them with it. "My soul gladly and hopefully took its rest," Hilary of Poitiers wrote, "and feared so little the interruption of death, that death seemed only a name for eternal life."[138]

If death is just another name for life, what is there to fear? In this chapter, we have seen men and women who boldly faced concentration camps, wild beasts, emperors, and entire political regimes. But what about cancer? A terrorist attack? The stock market collapsing? Or a natural disaster? None of these things, real as they are, can change what is true. If we have been buried with Christ, we will surely live with him. We are alive in the tomb. Fearless.

"Even though I walk through the valley of the shadow of death, I will fear no evil, for you are with me" (Psalm 23:4).

We may live in uncertain times, but this is all the more reason to let the Nicene Creed settle in your heart. Become like Christ in his death by *crucifying* your passions and desires until you embody the same character he did and others start to see him living through you. Share in his *sufferings,* knowing that he is with you and his presence will empower you with the grace to endure. Be *buried* with him so that you might rise with him far above every doubt and fear.

There is only one sentence left in the second article of the Nicene Creed. It takes us from earth to heaven, where Christ "sits at the right hand of the Father," inviting us to follow him.

"Be heavenly not only in hope, but also in conduct."

—LEO THE GREAT

11

ROSE AGAIN

*"If then you have been raised with Christ,
seek the things that are above, where Christ is."*
(Colossians 3:1)

A young girl hurried down the aisle of a parish church after Mass. "Father," she asked of the priest, "how do I get to heaven?" The priest thought for a moment then replied with a smile, "Follow the one who came from heaven and went back to heaven. He knows the way."

His answer was simple, one that any child could understand. Jesus doesn't just know the way; he is "the way" (John 14:6). *He came down from heaven to bring us up to heaven with him.* The Nicene Creed expounds on this theme,

> *Who for us men and for our salvation came down from heaven,
> . . . and was crucified for us. . . . And the third day He rose
> again, according to the Scriptures; and ascended into heaven,
> and sits at the right hand of the Father.*

The Son of God "came down," "rose again," and "ascended into heaven." In a sermon on the Feast of the Ascension, Leo the Great explained what it means to believe these things, "By this path of love whereby Christ came down to us, we too may mount up to Him."[139] Leo isn't talking about "going to heaven someday." His subject is *the daily process of rising to where Christ is by growing in the characteristics that he embodied in coming down to us.* Paul said the same to the Colossians,

> If then you have been raised with Christ, seek the things that are above, where Christ is, seated at the right hand of God. Set your minds on things that are above, not on things that are on earth. For you have died, and your life is hidden with Christ in God. When Christ who is your life appears, then you also will appear with him in glory. (Colossians 3:1–4)

If you are reading this, then you are not in heaven. But your thoughts, actions, and desires—your very life—can be, to the degree that you rise with Christ above the cares of this world and become *heavenly minded.* "It is in our mind . . . that we rise [with Christ]," Tertullian said, "since it is by this alone that we are as yet able to reach to heavenly objects."[140]

The day will come when "the trumpet will sound, and the dead will be raised imperishable, and we shall be changed" (1 Corinthians 15:52). But what about today? How do we rise above workplace or family drama? How can we keep our eyes and hands clean when temptations abound? How do we remain true to our convictions when everything around us only serves to contradict them? Such actions require another resurrection—one that occurs within our hearts and minds long before the last trumpet sounds.

Like the other events of Christ's passion, the Resurrection is meant to be contemplated and experienced until it becomes our own. Augustine said it best, "The resurrection of the body of the Lord is shown to belong to the mystery of our own inner resurrection."[141]

RESURRECTION MORNING

It was just before dawn. Sabbath was over, and Mary Magdalene was making her way through the hushed streets of Jerusalem to the place where they buried her Lord. The smell of myrrh and cassia mingled in the crisp morning air. Mary was going to anoint Jesus' body, carrying the fragrant spices with her.

It was the last time she would see him.

The sun was just below the horizon when Mary entered the garden. But even in the pale light, she could see that something was different from the Friday before. The stone that sealed the tomb was off to one side. The soldiers the governor instructed to stand guard were nowhere to be found.

Her heart sank.

Mary dropped the spices in her arms and started to run down the garden path. She reached the grave a few moments later and stooped down to look inside.

The tomb was empty.

Who had moved Jesus' body? Where would they take him? Why? Questions flooded Mary's mind and tears ran down her face.

A twig snapped and Mary jumped. She turned with a start and noticed the shadowy figure of a young man walking through the garden toward her. "Why are you crying?" he inquired.

Had she seen him before? Mary wasn't sure. She wiped the tears from her eyes and gathered the courage to ask, "Were you the one who took him away?"

The man didn't answer her question. He responded with a single word—"Mary"—and something in his tone caused her to recognize who it was. This was no grave-robber or gardener. It was Jesus—risen from the dead.

"Teacher!" she exclaimed, running to embrace him. But Jesus stopped her short. "Don't touch me, Mary," he said gently. "For I have not yet ascended to the Father; but go to my brothers and say to them, 'I am ascending to my Father and your Father, to my God and your God'" (John 20:17).

OUR FATHER

Why did Jesus say these words at this moment? It was Easter morning. He was alive—you'd think *that* would be the message he had for his disciples. Instead, Jesus repeated a principle that he first taught years before in the Lord's Prayer: God is "our Father in heaven" (Matthew 6:9).

Believing in "one God, the *Father* Almighty" is important—it is the very first phrase of the Nicene Creed—but what does it have to do with the Resurrection? Gregory of Nyssa said that Jesus' response to Mary on that first Easter morning "sums up the whole aim of his dispensation as man."[142] In other words, God became flesh, died, and rose again "to make . . . that true Father, from whom you were separated, to be your Father, and . . . to make that true God from whom you had revolted to be your God."[143] John of Damascus said it this way, "For by nothing else except the cross of our Lord Jesus Christ . . . [are] we made children and heirs of God. By the cross all things have been set aright."[144]

The Resurrection restored our relationship with God to the way it was always intended—like long lost children coming home.

But compare John 20:17 with what we have already seen in the Nicene Creed: "[We believe] in one Lord Jesus Christ, the Son of God, the only-begotten." If God is *our* Father, how is Christ the *only*-begotten? If "calling God his own Father" made Jesus "equal with God" (John 5:18) what does that mean for us as "sons of God, through faith" (Galatians 3:26)? *Are we equal with God?*

Of course not. "None can compare with [God]" (Psalm 40:5). But the ancient church taught something almost as scandalous: "[God] became Man that we might be made God."[145]

Athanasius wrote these controversial words in his book *On the Incarnation*. He also helped write the Nicene Creed and only "believed in one God." So when Athanasius said we can be "made God," he doesn't mean that we become God by nature, but rather *godly* through grace. Yes, we are human and make mistakes. But after the Resurrection, God can be our Father as truly as he is Jesus' Father. Cyril of Jerusalem beautifully explained how this works,

> For he did not say, "I ascend to our Father," lest the creatures should be made fellows of the Only Begotten. Instead, he said, "My Father and your Father." He is in one way mine, by nature. He is, in another way, yours, by adoption. And again, "to my God and your God," in one way mine, as his true and only-begotten Son, and in another way yours, as his workmanship.[146]

Nothing had to change for Jesus to be the Son of God. He is God by nature. But a great deal must change for us to be God's sons and daughters. It is not simply a matter of calling him "Father." We must rise with him to his level.

> Even when we were dead in our trespasses, [God] made us alive together with Christ—by grace you have been saved—and raised us up with him and seated us with him in the heavenly places in Christ Jesus. (Ephesians 2:5–6)

> We were buried therefore with him by baptism into death, in order that, just as Christ was raised from the dead by the glory of the Father, we too might walk in newness of life. For if we have been united with him in a death like his, we shall certainly be united with him in a resurrection like his. (Romans 6:4–5)

We rise with Christ—not only after death but here and now to the extent that we "walk in newness of life."

NEW LIFE

There was a certain monk known for his exceptional devotion. One day a beautiful woman walked past the monastery where he lived, and upon seeing her, he broke into tears. The other monks tried to comfort him, assuming that he had fallen into temptation, but he replied that his tears were tears of joy. He was in awe of the God who created such exceptional beauty. The brothers were astonished and ashamed. Praising God wasn't the first thought that entered their minds.

After relating this anecdote in his book, *The Ladder of Divine Ascent*, John Climacus explained the moral of the story, "Something that could have brought low one person managed to be the cause of a heavenly crown for another. If such a man feels and behaves in similar fashion on similar occasions, then he has already risen to immortality before the general resurrection."[147] This is what Augustine meant by "our own inner resurrection." *It is in our thoughts, feelings, and behaviors that we demonstrate whether or not we have risen with Christ.*

When you forgive someone who doesn't deserve it, you rise with Christ. When you wait for or remain faithful to your spouse, you rise with Christ. When you refuse to gossip, you rise with Christ. When you stay true to your word, you rise with Christ. Such actions may not sound like resurrection, but they are. They require dying to one way of life and living to one entirely different. This is the theme of the sixth chapter of Romans,

> Now if we have died with Christ, we believe that we will also live with him. We know that Christ, being raised from the dead, will never die again; death no longer has dominion over him. For the death he died he died to sin, once for all, but the life he lives he lives to God. So you also must consider yourselves dead to sin and alive to God in Christ Jesus. Let not sin therefore reign in your mortal body, to make you obey its passions. Do not present your members to sin as instruments for unrighteousness, but present yourselves to God as those who have been brought from death to life. (Romans 6:8–13)

In a sermon on the same chapter, John Chrysostom said that dying to sin means "not obeying it in anything anymore" and being as "unmovable as a dead man" in respect to the passions.[148] If we have died with Christ and risen with him, then "virtue is easy."[149]

It may not always *feel* easy, of course, but this is the mindset that the New Testament encourages us to have. We have died and risen with Christ to a new and divine way of life—not by our own power or ability, but through the empowerment of the Holy Spirit, as we will see in the next chapter.

GOING UP

Incredible as rising with Christ is, the story doesn't stop there. Forty days after the Resurrection, Jesus "ascended into heaven" and in so doing, he took us with him.

> [Jesus] presented himself alive to them after his suffering by many proofs, appearing to them during forty days and speaking about the kingdom of God. . . . And when he had said these things, as they were looking on, he was lifted up, and a cloud took him out of their sight. And while they were gazing into heaven as he went, behold, two men stood by them in white robes, and said, "Men of Galilee, why do you stand looking into heaven? This Jesus, who was taken up from you into heaven, will come in the same way as you saw him go into heaven." (Acts 1:3, 9-11)

The Ascension is a short story, so short that it can feel like an afterthought. But take another look at what the angels said to the men and women who were there, "This Jesus, who was taken up from you into heaven, will come *in the same way* as you saw him go into heaven" (v. 11, emphasis added).

How did Jesus go into heaven? "In the same way" that he rose from the dead, died on the cross, healed the sick, walked on the water, was born of a virgin, and did everything else in the Gospels—as God in the flesh. Jesus appeared to his disciples after the Resurrection and said, "Touch me, and see. For a spirit does not have flesh and bones as you see that I have" (Luke 24:39). Think what this means. The same flesh that the disciples embraced is currently "seated at the right hand of Power" and will one day "come [again] with the clouds of heaven" (Mark 14:62). This point was not lost on the early church,

> He ascended, and with Him our body ascended also.[150]

> Our nature [is] seated at the right hand of God, and we [are] made children and heirs of God.[151]

> To the same nature to which it was said in Adam, "Thou art earth, and unto earth shall thou go," it is said in Christ, "sit Thou on My right hand."[152]

> Through Thy glorious Ascension Thou didst deify the flesh which Thou didst assume, and placed it on the throne at the Father's right hand.[153]

The Ascension is Christmas in reverse. Jesus "came down from heaven" alone. But when he "ascended into heaven," he "raised us up with him and seated us with him in the heavenly places" (Ephesians 2:6). "God is now on earth, and man in heaven; on every side all things commingle,"[154] Chrysostom marveled.

The ancient church took this literally. If they were "in Christ Jesus" (Romans 8:1), then they were currently seated with him in heaven. "Although he ascended alone," Augustine said, "we also ascend, because we are in him by grace. . . . The body as a unity cannot be separated from the head."[155] Long before death, they were already in heaven. Augustine explained how, "We cannot be in heaven, as he is on earth, by divinity, but in him, we can be there by love."[156]

How would your actions change if you believed you were already in heaven? Would you be so worried about what your neighbors think? Would you cut off someone on the freeway or in conversation because your time is more important than theirs? Would you be so distracted? Would the number of your friends or followers or subscribers really matter? Or would you silence your phone and take time to pray, or love the unlovely, or give without restraint? It is not enough to think about heaven once a week or at funerals. It must become our reality—more real for us than anything else.

As I was preparing the notes for this chapter over a year ago, I received a phone call that I wasn't expecting. It wasn't good news, and I didn't know what to do. So I went for a walk around my neighborhood, but it felt like I was somewhere between heaven and earth. Did I believe that Jesus "ascended into heaven" higher than anything I was facing? Was I convinced that he was "seated at the right hand of the Father" and that I was there with him—"far above all rule and authority and power and dominion, and above every name that is named" (Ephesians 1:20–21)? It took some time to calm down, but I realized that I did believe these things and that belief empowered me for what lay ahead. The situation didn't change. I did. I rose with Christ above it, and you can as well, as you allow the powerful truth of the Ascension to settle in your heart.

Remember what Paul wrote to the Colossians,

> If then you have been raised with Christ, seek the things that are above, where Christ is, seated at the right hand of God. Set your minds on things that are above, not on things that are on earth. (Colossians 3:1–2)

Seeking and setting our minds on heaven is a choice each of us must make, not once and for all, but moment by moment. Those who retrain the "eyes of their hearts" (Ephesians 1:18) to look up and see what their physical eyes cannot, will become, in the words of Leo the Great, "heavenly not only in hope, but also in conduct."[157] Cyprian of Carthage said it this way,

> If we have raised our eyes from earth to heaven, if we have lifted our hearts, filled with God and Christ, to things above and divine, let us do nothing but what is worthy of God and Christ.... For this is to change what you had been, and to begin to be what you were not, that the divine birth might shine forth in you, that... God may be glorified in man.[158]

THE KINGDOM WITHIN

After the Ascension, there is one phrase left in the second article of the Nicene Creed. It took seven chapters for us to explore what the early church managed to say in a single paragraph.

The second article begins with who Jesus is: The "one Lord" to whom we must give account, the only "Light" by which we see, and "true God" together with the Father and the Holy Spirit.

Then it describes what Jesus did for our salvation. He "came down from heaven," "was incarnate" but not carnal, and "became man" but not a sinner, empowering us to follow in his steps. He was born of "the Holy Spirit and the Virgin Mary" and can be formed anew in us as we cooperate with his grace. Though fully God, he was "crucified," "suffered," and was "buried." Though fully man, he "rose again" three days later, annihilating the fear of death and raising us with him to a different kind of life. He "ascended into heaven" and even now is drawing us up toward himself where he "sits at the right hand of the Father."

The second article concludes with what Jesus *will* do,

> *He shall come again with glory to judge the living and the dead; whose Kingdom shall have no end.*

There is more about "the life of the world to come" in the Nicene Creed so we will save everything about the future for the final chapter. But there is a dimension of "whose Kingdom shall have no end" that directly relates to our present subject.

> Now when He [Jesus] was asked by the Pharisees when the kingdom of God would come, He answered them and said, "The kingdom of God does not come with observation; nor will they say, 'See here!' or 'See there!' For indeed, the kingdom of God is within you." (Luke 17:20-21, NKJV)

The religious leaders of Jesus' day were so focused on their preconceptions about heaven that they missed the real thing. Jesus had to direct their attention inward—away from prophetic signs and geopolitics to within their own hearts and minds. Cyril of Alexandria paraphrased this warning, which is just as pertinent for us today,

> Do not ask about the times in which the season of the kingdom of heaven will again arise and come. Rather, be eager that you may be found worthy of it. It is within you. That is, it depends on your own wills and is in your own power, whether or not you receive it.[159]

Sometimes the fear of "earning our way" to heaven prevents us from taking the time and effort to develop the kingdom within. This goes back to the distinction between earning and effort discussed in Chapter Nine. Paul wrote that there are those who "will be saved, but only as through fire" (1 Corinthians 3:15), that is, nothing they did in this life was of eternal significance. On the other hand, Jesus said that, "Those who are considered worthy to attain to that age and to the resurrection from the dead ... cannot die anymore, because they are equal to angels and are sons of God, being sons of the resurrection" (Luke 20:35-36). What a difference. Is the goal to get into heaven by the skin of our teeth or to become sons and daughters of the resurrection by developing the kingdom within?

The choice is ours.

In his all-time classic, *Conferences,* John Cassian wrote, "The objective of our life is the kingdom of God, but we should carefully ask what we should aim for."[160] That is, heaven may be our final destination, but getting there cannot be our focus.

> The aim of our profession is the kingdom of God or the kingdom of heaven. But our point of reference, our objective, is a clean heart, without which it is impossible for anyone to reach our target. . . . Everything we do, our every objective, must be undertaken for the sake of this purity of heart.[161]

What does Cassian mean by doing everything for "purity of heart?" It is more than keeping ourselves "unstained from the world" (James 1:27), though behavior has something to do with it. Think of a farmer or businessman. One desires a harvest, the other wants a healthy bottom line, but neither will achieve their goal without singleness of mind. The farmer doesn't hope for a harvest; his life is the harvest. It is why he buys seed, tills the soil, wakes up early, and stays out late. It is why the businessman buys when others sell and sells when others buy. Both delay temporary gratification for future hope. Their actions and lifestyles become a "foretaste of what they hope to . . . enjoy one day."[162]

So it is with us. "The aim of our profession is the kingdom of God" but our daily objective, our foretaste of heaven, is "purity of heart." A clean conscience. Complete devotion. Singlemindedness. "Blessed are the pure in heart, for they shall see God" (Matthew 5:8). Heaven is the prize, but purity of heart is what we pursue. In so doing, we develop the kingdom within and begin, with feet still planted on earth, to ascend to where Christ is and realize his life in us.

> Who shall ascend the hill of the Lord?
> And who shall stand in his holy place?
> He who has clean hands and a pure heart,
> Who does not lift up his soul to what is false
> And does not swear deceitfully.

He will receive blessing from the Lord

And righteousness from the God of his salvation. (Psalms 24:3–5)

For John Cassian and countless others, "purity of heart" summarizes the entire Christian experience. "[We] have purity of heart for an objective and eternal life as the goal."[163]

The Nicene Creed has more to say about this life, specifically, the one who gives it—the third person of the Trinity, "the Holy Spirit, the Lord, the Giver of Life."

"It is eternal life

to know

the Holy Spirit."

—AMBROSE OF MILAN

12

GIVER OF LIFE

"The one who sows to the Spirit will from the Spirit reap eternal life."
(Galatians 6:8)

"I baptize you into Christ, in the name of the Father, Son, and Holy Spirit."

That was my cue. After the pastor said these words, I took a deep breath as he took my hand and gently guided me down into the water. Everything was silent for a moment or two; then I came up out of the water to the roar of applause. Everyone in the church was on their feet, clapping, smiling, shouting, and looking right at me.

Your experience may be very different, but for me, being baptized at the age of nine was one of the most memorable events of my childhood. I can still remember standing waist-deep in the water, looking out at my family, friends, and people I barely knew. There was so much joy on their faces and excitement over what I had done.

But what had I done? I was a baptized Christian, but what did that mean apart from getting wet? How was I baptized in the name of, or *into* "the Father, Son, and Holy Spirit?"

I wasn't even quite sure who they were.

I knew the Father. My dad loved and cared for me and being his son helped me understand what God must be like. I knew the Son. Jesus was the one I heard stories about and colored pictures of every week in Sunday school. But the Holy Spirit? The only reference I had for the "Holy Ghost," as we often called him, was a bedsheet covered with holes like the one Charlie Brown wore in the Halloween special that I watched with my family every October. There are far better ways to imagine the Holy Spirit—the New Testament depicts him "like a dove" (John 1:32) descending from heaven and "divided tongues as of fire" (Acts 2:2) above the apostles' heads—but even this language is symbolic and difficult to nail down.

As a nine-year-old boy, I believed in the Father and the Son, but the Holy Spirit remained a mystery.

And so he is for many of us. Today, there are as many opinions on the Holy Spirit as there are denominations. Some of us don't know what to do with him and neglect his presence. Others so emphasize a particular aspect of his character—how he leads us, fills us, makes us holy, or helps us pray—that we miss who the Spirit is at the most basic level.

God.

The Holy Spirit is the third person of the Trinity—just as real, just as divine, and just as essential to the Christian faith as the Father and the Son. This is the point of the third article of the Nicene Creed,

> [We believe] in the Holy Spirit, the Lord, the Giver of Life, who proceeds from the Father; who with the Father and the Son together is worshipped and glorified; who spoke by the prophets.

Like the first two articles, the third article examines the nature of divinity. *Is the Holy Spirit God?* The Creed answers *yes* in several different ways,

» The Holy Spirit spoke as God to the prophets of old. What he said is recorded as the word of God in the scriptures.

» The Holy Spirit is worshipped and honored as God by all Christians.

» The Holy Spirit proceeds from the Father and shares the same divinity with him.

» The Holy Spirit is the Lord of all.

These are excellent answers—to a question that few ask today. Most of the contemporary debate about the Holy Spirit is over what he does, not who he is. But for the ancient church, these concepts were inseparable. The divinity of the Holy Spirit meant everything to the earliest Christians.

In a word, it gave them *life*.

Before mentioning worship or the scriptures or anything else, the Nicene Creed identifies the Holy Spirit as "the Lord, the *Giver of Life*." For centuries, this phrase was key to understanding not only the Holy Spirit, but also the Father, the Son, and the entire Christian experience.

What kind of life does the Spirit give? How do we receive it? And what effect should it have on our lives? So much could, and should, be said about the Holy Spirit, but as we explore this simple phrase, we will rediscover that beautiful—and uniquely Christian—way of life described by Paul,

> "It is no longer I who live, but Christ who lives in me" (Galatians 2:20).

LIFE IN ALL ITS DIMENSIONS

Only God can give life.

According to the scriptures, God "breathed the breath of life" (Genesis 2:7) into Adam and the same "breath of the Almighty gives us life" (Job 33:4). If the Holy Spirit gives or "creates" life, as some versions of the Creed word it, then the Spirit is God and should be "worshipped and glorified" as such. But "Life" is capitalized in the Creed, and it meant so much more to the men who wrote it than the breath in their lungs,

> For the one who sows to his own flesh will from the flesh reap corruption, but the one who sows to the Spirit will from the Spirit reap eternal life. (Galatians 6:8)

As Christians, we reap, or receive, *eternal* life from the Holy Spirit. But in this context and throughout the New Testament, "eternal" isn't a duration as much as it is a quality or kind of life. Consider the opening of 1 John,

> That which was from the beginning, which we have heard, which we have seen with our eyes, which we looked upon and have touched with our hands, concerning the word of life—the life was made manifest, and we have seen it, and testify to it and proclaim to you the eternal life, which was with the Father and was made manifest to us. (1 John 1:11-2)

Think what John is saying. He touched eternal life with his hands and saw eternal life with his eyes. For the first disciples, eternal life wasn't some future hope; it was the daily experience of being with Christ. "He is the true God and eternal life" (1 John 5:20).

And how did the disciples touch and see eternal life? Through the Holy Spirit. "Do not fear to take Mary as your wife," the angel reassured Joseph, "for that which is conceived in her is *from the Holy Spirit*" (Matthew 1:20, emphasis added). This means that there is no virgin birth, and therefore no God made visible or touchable, apart from the Spirit. He is, in the words of Ambrose, the "Author of the Lord's Incarnation."[164]

But it doesn't stop there. The Holy Spirit is also the author of another incarnation—our own. He formed Christ in Mary two thousand years ago and is still forming Christ in each of us today,

> And we all, with unveiled face, beholding the glory of the Lord, are being transformed into the same image from one degree of glory to another. For this comes from the Lord who is the Spirit. (2 Corinthians 3:18)

Whether it feels like it or not, you are being transformed into the image of Jesus Christ. Not a similar image. "The same image." If this sounds impossible, that's because it is—at least from a merely human perspective. The transformation taking place inside you right now, empowering you to *be* like Christ and not just believe in him, is the work of the Holy Spirit. "It is God who works in you," Paul marveled, "both to will and to work for his good pleasure" (Philippians 2:13). The life that the Spirit gives you, leading you "from one degree of glory to another," is his own—the divine life of God himself.

For the ancient church, this was absolute proof of the Holy Spirit's divinity. No one "can give life eternal who is not true God,"[165] Ambrose said. Gregory Nazianzus went even further, "How could he not be God ... by whom you also become god?"[166]

"Becoming god" is a statement that we have encountered before. And while it sounds controversial, remember who said it—men like Gregory, Athanasius,[167] Augustine,[168] John of Damascus,[169] and countless other "greats" from the Christian past. None of them meant that we are, or ever could become, the "one God, the Father Almighty." And yet they dared to believe what the scriptures plainly teach: We can share in the same divine life as we receive it from the Holy Spirit—and that life doesn't just forgive us or take us to heaven one day. It makes us like him.

Or at least it should. We all know Christians who look nothing like Christ—for whom the life of God has little or no discernable effect. The Holy Spirit gives life. The question is, *How do we receive the life that the Spirit gives?*

The answer requires getting wet.

LIVING WATER—FOR REALLY LIVING

It was a sunny day in Malibu. My wife and I were driving up Pacific Coast Highway en route to the beach when a roadside stand came into view. "Stand" is generous. It was more like a run-down, white van with the words "Bonsai for sale" plastered on the side.

We would have kept driving, but our coffee table at home was looking a little bare, so we pulled over and picked up a tiny juniper in a ceramic pot. Our record with houseplants wasn't great, but the proprietor reassured us. "Water it once a month," he smiled as he took our money, "and this tree will outlive you."

That was August. By October, our beautiful bonsai was brown, withered, and covered with gnats.

What happened? We watered it at least twice.

When we took our dying tree to a local greenhouse, the gardener shook her head. A bonsai should never be dry, she informed us. It must be watered continuously—once a day, not once a month.

We should have known better, but our first of many failed attempts at horticulture illustrates a principle that applies to people as well as plants: *Growth requires something outside ourselves*. For a bonsai, it's water. For us, it's the Holy Spirit.

This is the context of John Chapter 4. The story is a familiar one: Jesus asks a woman at a well for a drink of water. When she is surprised by his request, he replies,

> If you knew . . . who it is that is saying to you, "Give me a drink," you would have asked him, and he would have given you living water. . . . Everyone who drinks of this water will be thirsty again, but whoever drinks of the water that I will give him will never be thirsty again. The water that I will give him will become in him a spring of water welling up to eternal life. (John 4:10, 13-14)

A few chapters later, Jesus explains what this "living water" is, or rather, *who* it is,

> On the last day of the feast, the great day, Jesus stood up and cried out, "If anyone thirsts, let him come to me and drink. Whoever believes in me, as the Scripture has said, 'Out of his heart will flow rivers of living water.'" Now this he said about the Spirit, whom those who believed in him were to receive, for as yet the Spirit had not been given, because Jesus was not yet glorified. (John 7:37–39)

In these passages, Jesus calls the Holy Spirit "water." Why? Did the woman at the well need her sins washed away? Yes, but Jesus' word choice—"rivers of *living* water," "a spring of water welling up to eternal *life*"—hint at something beyond forgiveness. The woman's personal life was a mess. She had been through five broken marriages and was heading toward a sixth.[170] She was the spiritual equivalent of our bonsai—dry and dying.

And yet Jesus looked at her with more compassion than the gardener looked at us. He offered her a drink of the Holy Spirit. If she took it, the Spirit wouldn't just clean her up or wash her off. He would change her from within and, like water to a seed, transform her into something beautiful.

GROWING UP

In his commentary on John 4, Cyril of Jerusalem used the same imagery of water to describe the effect of the Holy Spirit on each of our lives,

> Why did He [Jesus] call the grace of the Spirit water? Because by water all things subsist; because water brings forth grass and living things; because the water of the showers comes down from heaven; because it comes down one in form, but works in

many forms. For . . . one and the same rain comes down upon all the world, yet it becomes white in the lily, and red in the rose, and purple in violets and hyacinths and different and varied in each several kind . . . for the rain does not change itself, and come down first as one thing, then as another, but adapting itself to the constitution of each thing which receives it, it becomes to each what is suitable. Thus also the Holy Ghost, being one, and of one nature, and indivisible, divides to each His grace, according as He will: and as the dry tree, after partaking of water, puts forth shoots, so also the soul in sin, when it has been through repentance made worthy of the Holy Ghost, brings forth clusters of righteousness.[171]

What a powerful image of grace. The Holy Spirit is like rain coming down from heaven. We respond like wildflowers, drinking in the rain and "growing up in every way into him" (Ephesians 4:15).

But how does a flower or any other plant grow? By absorbing carbon dioxide through its leaves and water through its roots. We call this process "photosynthesis" since these elements combine, or synthesize, with light inside the plant and cause it to grow. In the same way, Jesus promised that the Holy Spirit "will become *in us* a spring of water welling up to eternal life" (John 4:14, emphasis added). We are changed from the inside, as our lives become saturated with eternal life. The early church called this process *theosis* rather than photosynthesis, but the mechanics are the same. We become like God through union with him—continually drawing from and relying on the source of life in whatever situation we may face.

Earlier this week, a friend said some things about me that were unwarranted, and, frankly, unchristian. I tried to forget what was said and move on, but days later, his words were still repeating in my mind. I couldn't let them go.

This is also the week before Easter, and my wife and I have spent the last month and a half preparing to celebrate the Resurrection as the church always has: with prayer and fasting. Fasting isn't easy, but forgiveness is harder. And I knew I hadn't forgiven this person. I responded in kindness because I dislike confrontation, but I was boiling on the inside. I cared what he thought about me. I wanted to vindicate myself and my character. I felt like punching him in the nose.

It went on like this for a day or two until I remembered a line from Augustine, "When you are commanded by the law to do something, ask the Spirit to help you."[172] What I needed to do was obvious—forgive—but I couldn't find the strength to do it. So I asked. And the Spirit helped. It wasn't a holiday that I was preparing for. It was this moment—an opportunity, however small, to live the life of my Lord. With the help of the Holy Spirit, I prayed from my heart the prayer from the cross, "Father, forgive him,"[173] and tapped into a source of life far greater than my own.

Maybe you don't need the strength to forgive as I did. Maybe what you need is patience toward a loved one, courage to stand up for what is right, willpower to break an old habit, or hope in the face of tragedy and loss. The Holy Spirit gives life, especially when ours comes up short. He causes us to grow up into Christ in ways that are unique to each of us. This is what Cyril meant when he said that, "One and the same rain . . . becomes white in the lily, and red in the rose, and purple in violets and hyacinths."[174]

The Holy Spirit may look different in you than he does in me. Some of us may grow faster or taller or have more "fruit," but the same Spirit transforms each of us into what we could never be on our own. We become what the Holy Spirit is—holy—until "our lives are a Christ-like fragrance rising up to God" (2 Corinthians 2:15).

Of course, no flower grows overnight. Growth is a process that takes time, sometimes a lifetime, but every process starts somewhere. Gregory Nazianzus described the starting point for every Christian in his profoundly controversial style, "I have put on Christ, I have been transformed into Christ by Baptism."[175]

BAPTIZED INTO CHRIST AND HIS LIFE

After establishing what it means to believe in the Holy Spirit as the "Giver of Life," the Nicene Creed continues with the fourth and final article,

> [We believe] in one Holy, Catholic, and Apostolic Church. I acknowledge one baptism for the remission of sins. I look for the resurrection of the dead, and the life of the world to come. Amen.

It may sound like the Creed is changing subjects, but it's not. These three themes—church, baptism, and the Holy Spirit—go together in scripture,

> [Be] eager to maintain the unity of the Spirit in the bond of peace. There is one *body* and one *Spirit*—just as you were called to the one hope that belongs to your call—one Lord, one faith, one *baptism*. (Ephesians 4:3-5, emphasis added)

> For in one *Spirit* we were all *baptized* into one *body*—Jews or Greeks, slaves or free—and all were made to drink of one Spirit. (1 Corinthians 12:13, emphasis added)

When Jesus said, "If anyone thirsts, let him come to me and drink" (John 7:37), the first Christians understood this invitation in a specific way. We "come" to Christ by becoming part of his body—the church—and we "drink" by receiving the Holy Spirit at baptism.

Church and *baptism* may not be words that you want to hear. They mean different things to different people, and often bring back bad memories of those who hurt us, institutions that made us feel alone, or rituals that we didn't understand.

For others, these words have the opposite effect and are among the most cherished in the Creed. At this point, most commentaries focus on the so-called four marks of the church—that the body of Christ is "One,"

"Holy," "Catholic," and "Apostolic." And while these things are true, necessary, and life-changing to believe, the issue of how and why we "do church" will have to wait for another day.

Instead, let's consider the Creed's statements on "one Church" and "one baptism" in light of what we have already seen about the Holy Spirit as the "Giver of Life." From this perspective, the church is the *place* where the Holy Spirit gives life through "the apostles' teaching," "fellowship," "breaking of bread," and "prayers" (Acts 2:42). Baptism is *how* we enter the church and the first *way* that the Holy Spirit gives us his life. Despite our various, and sometimes contradictory, experiences of these things, the church and baptism are tangible realities that exist to help us grow up into Christ.

So why doesn't it always feel that way? Particularly in the case of baptism, an act that many Christians either don't remember or have never experienced, this seems like a bit of a stretch. How can a little water make us "taste the heavenly gift," "share in the Holy Spirit," and experience "the powers of the age to come" (Hebrews 6:5)? It can't. Jesus said as much to the woman at the well. And yet, Jesus told Nicodemus that water could do all this and more. We are born again by *"water* and the Spirit" (John 3:5, emphasis added)—not by the Spirit alone. Ambrose of Milan explained this seeming contradiction,

> If, then, there be any grace in the water, it is not from the nature of water, but from the presence of the Holy Spirit. Do we live in the water or in the Spirit? Are we sealed in the water or in the Spirit? For in Him we live.[176]

Baptism is the point of contact with the Holy Spirit where he gives us our first drink of eternal life. But it's up to us to live it, or baptism is just a bath. In the introduction to his *Catechetical Lectures*, Cyril of Jerusalem warned candidates for baptism not to be like Simon Magus, the magician whom Philip baptized but Peter rebuked for trying to "obtain the gift of God with money" (Acts 8:20),

> Even Simon Magus once came to the Laver of Baptism, he was baptized, but not enlightened. His body he dipped in water, but admitted not the Spirit to illuminate his heart. His body went down and came up; but his soul was not buried together with Christ, nor with Him raised.[177]

I was nine when I was baptized, but the point of baptism isn't how or when it happens. It's living as if it happened. It's "putting on" and "being transformed into Christ"[178] as Gregory Nazianzus said. This is how we truly become members of the church—the one, living body of Jesus Christ. But if that is the case, why the water or the ritual at all?

Before Jesus ascended into heaven, he gave instructions concerning baptism in a passage commonly known as the Great Commission,

> Go therefore and make disciples of all nations, baptizing them in the name of the Father and of the Son and of the Holy Spirit, teaching them to observe all that I have commanded you. And behold, I am with you always, to the end of the age. (Matthew 28:19-20)

Baptism in water requires us to receive the faith, particularly the doctrine of the Trinity, from someone else. Ananias baptized Paul.[179] John baptized Jesus.[180] *You can't baptize yourself.* Each of us, in the words of John Cassian, are "initiated into the truth ... by the fathers."[181] We receive the faith from those who went before us, which of course, is the reason for the church.

And for the Creed.

The Nicene Creed was originally a baptismal formula. It was taught to candidates for baptism and recited at baptism, and how I wish I knew the Creed before I "took the plunge." So many of my questions about God would have been answered. I would have been able to focus on living my faith from the moment I came out of the water rather than spending years trying to figure it out on my own.

The Creed contains what we must believe about the Father, Son, and the Holy Spirit before we can share in their life. We don't recite these truths or go through these motions because that's what Christians do. We believe these things to begin to comprehend the incredible transformation that is taking place within us. We do these things to submerge ourselves in the truth and take part in our own transformation. "Let us be baptized, then, that we may be victorious," Gregory Nazianzus said. "Let us participate in the purifying waters."[182]

But Baptism is only the beginning. The triumphant, final phrase of the Nicene Creed promises far more in the Christian life to look forward to.

*"The final sequel

of man's life and death

is the resurrection."*

—HILARY OF POITIERS

13

LOOKING FORWARD

*"This light momentary affliction is preparing
for us an eternal weight of glory beyond all comparison."*
(2 Corinthians 4:17)

Spoiler alert.

If this phrase appears in a review for a movie you haven't seen, chances are you'll stop reading. When it comes to popular entertainment, no one wants to know what is coming next. The unknown is what keeps us glued to the screen and on the edge of our seats.

Real life is a different story. We want to know what is coming and ask question after question to that effect: What does the future hold? What happens after death? What about heaven? Or hell? So far we have steered clear of subjects like these and focused on what the Nicene Creed means for us here and now. But the Creed isn't only concerned with the present. It contains some "spoilers" of its own,

> He [Jesus] shall come again with glory to judge the living and the dead; whose Kingdom shall have no end.

> *I look for the resurrection of the dead, and the life of the world to come. Amen.*

These are the last lines of the second and fourth articles of the Nicene Creed and the final statements that we will cover in this book. They give away the conclusion of the Christian faith—something that scholars call *eschatology*, from the Greek word for "end."

Whether it is a happy ending depends on who you ask. For some, every news cycle foretells doom, gloom, and the end of the world. There may be light at the end of the tunnel, but the darkness gets all the attention. Others shake their heads, roll their eyes, and explain away so much that there is no future left to believe in.

Early Christians had a different vision of the end and reminded each other of it whenever they recited the Creed. Christ will return in glory. Righteousness will be rewarded. Empires and administrations will rise and fall, but Christ's kingdom will never end. There is a world to come and a life that even death cannot extinguish.

In the Creed, the future is bright. It is something to look forward to.

LIVING LIKE WE BELIEVE

The purpose of the Nicene Creed is to summarize what "we believe" about the Father, Son, and Holy Spirit. In comparison with the nature of God himself, the things we believe about the future may seem less important. We might ask questions about the end, but it's not clear what to do with the answers. Does it matter that Christ's kingdom will "have no end" when whatever country we call home has its own laws to follow and taxes to pay? There may be a "resurrection of the dead," but our hearts still break when a loved one dies. Jesus said to "be ready" (Matthew 24:44) because he is "coming soon" (Revelation 22:20). That was almost two thousand years ago.

Some Christians believe end-times conspiracy theories. Others hardly believe in an end at all. Most of us fall somewhere in the middle. We acknowledge what the Creed says about the future, but are unsure what to do about it. None of these things make a difference in everyday life.

Or that's how it seems. In reality, what we believe—or don't believe—about the end affects everything we do.

If we believe that a day is coming where we must "give account for every careless word we speak" (Matthew 12:36) would we gossip, complain, or bend the truth? Would we make the same comments or post the same photos on social media?

If we believe that Christ will "rule all the nations" (Revelation 12:5), would we base our identity on a political party, age group, denomination, or skin color?

If we believe that we "will live, even after dying" (John 11:25, NLT) would we respond in the same way to an unfavorable doctor's diagnosis? Would we be so concerned with the cares of life, or would we live with eternity in mind?

The end matters. Despite all we don't know, these are essential truths to settle in our hearts.

Knowing what is coming next in a movie won't change the story, but it will affect how you view it. The same is true in life. Every position we hold and action we take says something about what we believe is coming next. Instead of wondering what to do while waiting for Christ's return or the resurrection of the dead, ask yourself, *Am I living like I believe these things will happen?*

John Chrysostom said it like this,

> [We should] not deceive ourselves nor think that our fortunes begin and end with this present life. You see, even if many people don't admit this in so many words, but claim to believe in the doctrine of the resurrection and future retribution, nevertheless I take notice not of their words but of what they

do day by day. That is to say, if you are looking forward to resurrection and retribution, why go chasing the values of this life to such an extent?[183]

We can say we believe that Christ "will come again in glory" or that there is a "world to come," but we prove through what we "do day by day" whether we believe these things. Are you worried about tomorrow, or confident that even if "heaven and earth pass away," God's promises will never fail (Matthew 24:32)? Do you spend your time, money, and talents to "lay up for yourself treasures on earth" or "treasures in heaven" (Matthew 6:20)? Will you do whatever it takes to get ahead? Or do you believe that one day "each of us will give an account of himself to God" (Romans 14:12) and act accordingly? "Let us set our thoughts on the future and give close attention to our lifestyle,"[184] Chrysostom concluded.

If the lifestyles of the earliest Christians are different than ours, it's not because they lived in a simpler time before smartphones or the internet. It's because they valued and looked forward to very different things than we do.

"My hope," Paul said, "is in the resurrection of the dead" (Acts 23:6, NLT).

FUTURE HOPE

In Chapter Eleven, we explored "the mystery of our own inner resurrection"[185] and saw how it is possible to rise with Christ now in our thoughts and behaviors. Inner resurrection is essential to follow Christ, but it is not what Paul meant when he announced to a packed courtroom, "My hope is in the resurrection of the dead."

Paul was on trial for his faith. He faced the anger of a mob, years of imprisonment, and even a death sentence. But he looked beyond all these things to what was still far off—to a moment in time when "all who are in the tombs will hear his [Christ's] voice and come out" (John 5:28–29).

Paul's hope was in a literal, physical resurrection of the dead. The next time he stood trial, he explained this hope in greater detail,

> And now I stand here on trial because of my hope in the promise made by God to our fathers, to which our twelve tribes hope to attain, as they earnestly worship night and day. And for this hope I am accused by Jews, O king! Why is it thought incredible by any of you that God raises the dead? (Acts 26:6-8)

The resurrection wasn't just another thing Paul believed. It was the culmination of his entire belief system, the point of the Law and the Prophets, and the hope of all humanity. Paul was so convinced that the dead would live again that he didn't understand how anyone could think otherwise. "Why is it thought incredible by any of you that God raises the dead?" he marveled.

And yet, from a purely human perspective, the resurrection *is* incredible. It goes against everything we thought we knew. Death is final. This life is all there is. There is no reason to question such statements, except for one Man who claimed that if we believe in him, he "will raise us up on the last day" (John 6:40). No one took him seriously until he died and rose again three days later. Now, generation after generation of his followers have lived as he did—unafraid of death and hoping in "a better resurrection" (Hebrews 11:35, NKJV).

It is impossible to overstate the importance of "the resurrection of the dead" to the Christian faith. Without it, there is no Christianity,

> But if there is no resurrection of the dead, then not even Christ has been raised. And if Christ has not been raised, then our preaching is in vain and your faith is in vain.... And if Christ has not been raised, your faith is futile and you are still in your sins. Then those also who have fallen asleep in Christ have perished. If in Christ we have hope in this life

only, we are of all people most to be pitied. (1 Corinthians 15:13-14, 17-19)

John of Damascus went even further, "If there is no resurrection, there is no God and no providence, and all things are being driven and carried along by mere chance."[186]

These are strong words. Neither Paul nor John had to say them. They could have stopped with Jesus rising from the dead, but they didn't. "We know," Paul insisted, "that God, who raised the Lord Jesus, will also raise us with Jesus and present us to himself" (2 Corinthians 4:14, NLT). He continued a few verses later,

> So we do not lose heart. Though our outer self is wasting away, our inner self is being renewed day by day. For this light momentary affliction is preparing for us *an eternal weight of glory beyond all comparison.* (2 Corinthians 4:16–17, emphasis added)

This is what Paul was looking forward to. For the first Christians, resurrection meant more than rising from the dead. It meant rising different. Glorious. What Paul calls "an eternal weight of glory" here, he refers to as "a mystery" (1 Corinthians 15:51), "putting on immortality" (1 Corinthians 15:54), "bearing the image of the man of heaven" (1 Corinthians 15:49), and being "swallowed up by life" (2 Corinthians 5:4) in other places. "What we will be has not yet appeared," the apostle John admitted, "but we know that when he appears *we shall be like him*, because we shall see him as he is" (1 John 3:2, emphasis added).

The resurrection is the final step in the Incarnation. It is the moment where "Christ in us" is no longer "the hope of glory" to come (Colossians 1:27), but the attainment of that glory. When we see him, we will be like him. We will *become* him, in the same sense that "iron blending with fire becomes fire"[187] to borrow a line from Cyril of Jerusalem. This transformation is both spiritual and physical. What is buried as "a natural body . . . is raised a spiritual body" (1 Corinthians 15:44). Christ "transforms our lowly body to be like his glorious body" (Philippians 3:21). Hilary of Poitiers described the resurrection as "the final sequel of man's life and death" where "these bodies of earthly origin shall be exalted to the fashion of a higher nature, and conformed to the glory of the Lord's body."[188] And Leo the Great said it this way,

> The flesh of the saints . . . in reward for their humility will be changed in a happy resurrection, and clothed with the glory of immortality, in nothing now to act contrary to the spirit, and . . . in complete unity and agreement with the will of the soul. For then the outer man will be the peaceful and unblemished possession of the inner man: then the mind, engrossed in beholding God, will be hampered by no obstacles of human weakness.[189]

At this moment, there are still "human weaknesses" to deal with. Our bodies age and eventually pass away. Sometimes we are tired, or anxious, or irritable. We make mistakes. For many Christians, hoping in the resurrection means waiting for the day when God will change everything we don't like about ourselves. But for the ancient church, hoping in the resurrection was active, not passive. "I have suffered the loss of all things . . . that I may gain Christ," (Philippians 3:8) Paul said. He continued the same thought a few verses later, "That by any means possible I may *attain the resurrection* from the dead" (Philippians 3:11, emphasis added).

TRAINING FOR ETERNITY

How could Paul, or anyone else for that matter, "attain the resurrection"—the most impossible, and therefore *unattainable*, fact of the Christian faith? To answer that question, let me tell you about one of my good friends.

Danny wrestled in high school. Like most young men, he also loves to eat, and there is a particular steakhouse in Newport Beach that both of us enjoy. We have been there several times over the years, but not once during wrestling season. I sit at my desk most days, so splurging on dinner and dessert only affects my waistline. But someone who wrestles has to "make weight." For Danny, an extra pound or two could mean a different weight class or disqualification from a match. If it was wrestling season, I would find someone else to invite to dinner. I knew his answer would be *no*.

Danny had a goal. He wanted to see a certain number when he stood on the scale, but a number wasn't what he was aiming for. His goal was to win. And to win, as he often did, he had to make weight. So he curbed his appetites and made sacrifices to gain something better. He didn't diet. He lived to win.

So did the first Christians. "For ours is no trifling aim; eternal life is our object of pursuit," Cyril of Jerusalem wrote. He went on to paraphrase the last line of the Nicene Creed, "We are taught to believe, 'And in the life everlasting,' for which as Christians we are striving."[190] For Cyril and countless others, the resurrection wasn't just something to hope for. It was a goal to pursue—a prize to strive after,

> Do you not know that in a race all the runners run, but only one receives the prize? So run that you may obtain it. Every athlete exercises self-control in all things. They do it to receive a perishable wreath, but we an imperishable. So I do not run aimlessly; I do not box as one beating the air. But I discipline my body and keep it under control, lest after preaching to others I myself should be disqualified. (1 Corinthians 9:24-27)

> That I may know him and the power of his resurrection, and may share his sufferings, becoming like him in his death, that by any means possible I may attain the resurrection from the

dead. Not that I have already obtained this or am already perfect, but I press on to make it my own, because Christ Jesus has made me his own. Brothers, I do not consider that I have made it my own. But one thing I do: forgetting what lies behind and straining forward to what lies ahead, I press on toward the goal for the prize of the upward call of God in Christ Jesus. (Philippians 3:10-14)

Verses like these can be challenging. At face value, it sounds like there may not be a resurrection to look forward to unless we "attain" it. Unless we earn it. But earning isn't the point. It isn't even possible. "Running to obtain" and "pressing on toward . . . the prize" means having a goal and allowing that goal to transform our lives until it becomes who we are.

To be an athlete, Danny gave up things I didn't—time, comfort, dessert—and as a result, he has trophies that I don't and can beat me at almost any sport. In the same way, early Christians called themselves "athletes of Christ."[191] They lived with less, fasted, went to church every day, memorized the scriptures, and took sin seriously. Like spiritual athletes, they trained for eternity by "laying aside every weight and sin" so they could "run with endurance the race that was set before them" (Hebrews 12:1). From a modern perspective, it may seem like everyone from the past was trying to work their way into God's favor. But they weren't. They were "making weight"—giving up comfort and complacency for something far better than mere self-righteousness,

I have fought the good fight, I have finished the race, I have kept the faith. Henceforth there is laid up for me the crown of righteousness, which the Lord, the righteous judge, will award to me on that day, and not only to me but also to all who have loved his appearing. (2 Timothy 4:7-8)

Other scriptures identify the reward that awaits us as the "crown of life" (James 1:12, Revelation 2:10). The end of our faith, the prize worth fighting for, and the goal each of us are running toward is *being like Christ and sharing in his life*.

Christianity is a race with "the resurrection of the dead and the life of the world to come" as the finish line. While it is possible to cross the finish line without taking the time and effort to grow in the character of Christ, that is like running a marathon without training first. It will be exhausting. Life's ups and downs will wear you out. Your faith will fail when the heat is up or the pressure is on.

Endurance only comes with training. Training involves sweat, sacrifice, and determination—but it is worth it. Instead of praying for life to be easy, early Christians used whatever circumstances they found themselves in to train for eternity. "Know that when your faith is tested, your endurance has a chance to grow. So let it grow, for when your endurance is fully developed, you will be perfect and complete, needing nothing" (James 1:3-4, NLT).

It's not a matter of *if* your faith will be tested, but *when*. When you lose your job, your home, or someone you love, will you also lose heart? When all it takes to get ahead is one "white lie," will you do it? When your passions, desires, and appetites are screaming to be satisfied, will you give in? Or will you allow your endurance to grow and take one step closer to the finish line?

Every day there are opportunities to train for eternity. The resurrection may be a long way off, but that doesn't mean you should put it off. What you will enjoy *then*, you prepare for *now* through every decision you make. This requires changing your perspective on all of life. Even death.

DYING DAILY

By modern standards, ancient Christians had an unhealthy preoccupation with death. Paul claimed to "die every day" (1 Corinthians 15:31). John Climacus wrote that, "Just as bread is the most necessary of all foods, so the thought of death is the most essential of all works."[192] Some of the first Christian services were held in catacombs and churches were built around the bones of saints and martyrs. This all may sound creepy or morbid, but very early in our history, Christians discovered that the most effective way to train for eternity is the constant "remembrance of death."[193] And it wasn't just the ancients who thought this way. In 1976, the evangelist Billy Graham delivered a sermon entitled, *You Can Have Resurrection Life*. He said this,

> If a person is dead, you cannot expect anything from him. And if you don't expect anything from him, you will not be surprised nor disappointed at anything that happens. *The only thing a dead person needs is life!*[194]

If you truly believe that you "have died with Christ" (Romans 6:8) and continue to "die every day" (1 Corinthians 15:31) with him, then all you will need, all you will strive for, and all that will satisfy you is life. *Eternal life.*

"The remembrance of death" means looking inward, away *from* "the cares of the world and the deceitfulness of riches and the desires for other things" (Mark 4:19), and looking *to* matters of the heart. In light of eternity, the soul is all that matters,

> For what will it profit a man if he gains the whole world and forfeits his soul? Or what shall a man give in return for his soul? For the Son of Man is going to come with his angels in the glory of his Father, and then he will repay each person according to what he has done. (Matthew 16:26-27)

When testing or temptation comes, how will you respond? Will you do what feels good or what is best for your career or reputation? Or will you pause, look inside, and do what is best for your soul by telling the truth? Or having a right attitude? Or refusing to compromise your principles no matter the cost?

There is a "resurrection of the dead and the life of the world to come." Christians just happen to live like this is true.

A FINAL WORD

One word remains in the Nicene Creed, and chances are you have heard it many times before,

Amen.

The Nicene Creed is a prayer, just not the kind that many of us are used to. Rather than a laundry list of what we want God to do for us, the Creed is a prayer in the traditional sense. John Climacus described prayer like this,

> Prayer is future gladness, action without end, wellspring of virtues, source of grace, hidden progress, food of the soul, enlightenment of the mind, an axe against despair, hope demonstrated, sorrow done away with.... It is a mirror of progress, a demonstration of success, evidence of one's condition, the future revealed, a sign of glory.[195]

There are so many powerful statements here, but notice that one word appears twice—*progress.* Prayer is "hidden progress" and "a mirror of progress." It is both how you grow up into Christ and the measure of your growth. John wrote in another place, "Your prayer shows where you stand."[196]

If prayer is about progressing in the faith, then the Nicene Creed is one of the most powerful prayers you can pray. Apart from the scriptures themselves, nothing will give you a clearer picture of "where you stand" in your walk with Christ than the Nicene Creed. Good luck reciting all of the Bible every day, but each of us can rehearse the Creed throughout our day—on lunch break, at a stop light, in line at the Post Office. Whenever we do, it is like looking in a mirror. We remind ourselves of everything "we believe" but sometimes forget,

God made "all things visible and invisible," so I choose to look beyond what I can see with my physical eyes.

Jesus "was incarnate of the Holy Spirit and the Virgin Mary," so I can honor God in my flesh with the Spirit's help.

There is "the life of the world to come," so I won't be weighed down with the cares of this life.

The list goes on and on, but it isn't enough to remind ourselves of what "we believe" every once in a while. To truly settle in our hearts and minds, the Creed must become a practice—part of our daily routine.

I played the double bass as a teenager, and my teacher could always tell if I had practiced since my last lesson. When I did, I made progress on the piece of music he assigned. When I didn't, I fell behind and my playing suffered. Owning an instrument, the ability to read music, paying for lessons—none of these things made me a better musician.

Only practicing did.

Today, the Bible is more available than at any time in history. Going to church is easier than ever before. Billions of people identify as Christians. But are they, without the daily practice of being like Christ? *The one thing that makes a Christian a Christian is imitating Christ.* There is always an urge to qualify this statement. But as soon as we do, as soon as we lower the bar or make exceptions for ourselves, we abandon the ancient faith for a modern-day knock-off.

The practice of Christianity is called "discipleship," and from the day it was written, the Nicene Creed was *the* way of making disciples. Or at least it was until very recently in church history. You can spend decades in many modern churches and never know the Creed exists. Maybe we could get by without a Creed if we taught the same truths. But we don't. Sad to say, the tradition I come from, the evangelical world, has all but lost the beauty of the Incarnation, and along with it, the practice—the art—of Christian discipleship.

Will we remember what we once knew, embrace our Creed, and rekindle the fire that burned within those who practiced the ancient faith?

I believe we will, ironically, because of how many of my friends have left the church in recent years. Some have rejected the gospel, but not all. Many are just tired. Tired of services that are little more than concerts. Tired of being talked-down to or talked out of being like Christ. Tired of "life-changing" messages that they can't remember half an hour later. Tired of a gospel with no depth. Tired of a faith that they can't see or touch or feel. And so they leave the church *because* they believe.

They believe that God is bigger than who he is made out to be. They believe that the faith is older than those who preach it. They believe that right is right and wrong is wrong no matter which political party is in power. They believe that some questions deserve better answers than "pray more," "read the Bible," and "go to church." Eventually, our pews will be empty enough that those who remain will figure this out and start searching for solutions. That search will lead, as it always has, back to the tried and true faith that those who went before us knew and recorded for posterity in the Nicene Creed.

MY PRAYER

This isn't the only possible outcome, of course. My prayer is that we save ourselves the time and the trouble and remember our Creed before the situation gets that desperate. But whatever the immediate future holds, I am convinced that the day will come when the one Church will once more say with one voice, "We believe. . ." and, as G.K. Chesterton wrote, "the ancient Church" through her ancient Creed will "again startle the world with the paradoxes of Christianity."[197]

It has been almost a decade since I heard the sermon that changed my life and first encountered the Nicene Creed. In that time, I committed the Creed to memory, learned the original language it was written in, discovered it in the pages of scripture, and re-discovered it in the writings of the fathers. Still, the Creed feels brand new whenever I recite it and ponder what it says. The Nicene Creed, like the faith itself, is a paradox. It is taught to and believed by new Christians, yet our greatest theologians cannot plumb its depths. It takes moments to say, hours to memorize, years to learn, and a lifetime to fully experience its transforming power.

There will always be more to say about the Nicene Creed. The real challenge is to set down the book and take up the practice of being like Christ.

You have read the Creed. You have said the Creed. You have encountered the Creed throughout the rich Christian past. Now it is time, with all those who went before you, to live the Creed and prove by experience the transforming power of the timeless truths that "we believe."

Epilogue
WHY THE CREED?

I held my son, Peter, for the first time an hour after he was born. The moment his big, dark eyes made contact with mine, all the preparation and parenting classes went out the window. I had no idea what to do or say. And so, as I tend to do when words fail, I began to recite the Creed.

I have said the Nicene Creed countless times before and in more appropriate settings than a busy hospital room, but this time was different. *"We* believe"—"we" wasn't just my wife and me anymore. *"Only-begotten* of the *Father"* carried infinitely more weight. *"Made man"* brought me to tears. Here in my arms was my life, my character, my nature shared by someone else.

It was a private moment between father and son. My wife was resting. The nurses were bustling around the room. No one overheard what I said. It would have remained our little secret—until I shared the story with my writing coach, and he encouraged me to include it as a final thought at the end of this book.

Why the Creed? Of everything that I could have said to my newborn son, of all the ways to express my love for him, why these words at this moment?

The Nicene Creed is so precious to me. Yes, it is what I believe, but more importantly, it is how I choose to behave. And it's not just phrases like "judge the living and the dead" and "the life of the world to come" that keep me on the straight and narrow. "Visible and invisible" directs my focus. "Incarnate of the Holy Spirit and the Virgin Mary" helps me overcome temptation. "Giver of Life" encourages me to grow daily in the character of Christ. "I believe in the Church" challenges me to do one of the most difficult things in the Christian life—get along with other Christians.

I said the Creed to Peter on the day he was born and still say it to him whenever I give him a bottle or rock him to sleep, not because I want him to repeat rote words back to me one day, but because I want him to take every word personally and live each one from his heart. And that is why I wrote this book. You may never go to a church that recites the Creed every Sunday. Mine doesn't. You may never read the writings of the ancient church for yourself. I know few who have. The power of the Creed isn't idealizing the past or returning to an old way of doing things. It is reminding ourselves every day of all we believe so we can live and act like believers.

Like Christians.

My prayer for Peter and for you is that these timeless and trusted words will strengthen you, challenge you, and stay with you wherever you go.

THE NICENE CREED

*We believe in one God, the Father Almighty,
Maker of heaven and earth, and of all things visible and invisible.*

*And in one Lord Jesus Christ, the Son of God, the only-begotten,
begotten of the Father before all ages. Light of Light;
true God of true God; begotten, not made; of one essence
with the Father, by whom all things were made; who for us men
and for our salvation came down from heaven, and was incarnate
of the Holy Spirit and the Virgin Mary, and became man.
And He was crucified for us under Pontius Pilate, and suffered,
and was buried. And the third day He rose again, according to
the Scriptures; and ascended into heaven, and sits at the right
hand of the Father; and He shall come again with glory to judge
the living and the dead; whose Kingdom shall have no end.*

*And in the Holy Spirit, the Lord, the Giver of Life, who proceeds
from the Father; who with the Father and the Son together is
worshipped and glorified; who spoke by the prophets.*

*In one Holy, Catholic, and Apostolic Church. I acknowledge
one baptism for the remission of sins. I look for the resurrection
of the dead, and the life of the world to come. Amen.*

Published by the Orthodox Church in America
(https://oca.org/orthodoxy/the-orthodox faith/doctrine-scripture/the-symbol-of-faith/nicene-creed)

MARK NAUROTH is a writer, speaker, software developer, and avid student of the early church.

During a prolonged illness in his teens and early twenties, Mark developed a determination that led to a lifelong journey of self-education and entrepreneurship. In the decade since his full recovery, the software Mark authored through his consulting firm, Resident Genius, has helped his enterprise clients capture, grow, and manage hundreds of millions of dollars in revenue. Through his other venture, Worldview Guys, Mark directed, produced, and co-authored a thirteen-part documentary on the intersection of faith and culture acclaimed by Christian thought-leaders and enjoyed by churches across the United States.

In his spare time, Mark taught himself just enough Koine Greek "to be dangerous," plunged head-first into the writings of the church fathers, and is working on audio and video treatments of his favorite gems from the Christian past.

Mark was born and raised in Nebraska and currently resides with his wife and son in Southern California.

You can connect with Mark and learn more about the historic Christian faith at:

POWEROFTHECREED.COM

ENDNOTES

1. Vincent of Lérins, *The Commonitory of Vincent of Lérins* (Baltimore: Joseph Robinson, 1847), 5.
2. John Climacus, *The Ladder of Divine Ascent*, ed. Richard J. Payne, trans. Colm Luibheid and Norman Russell, The Classics of Western Spirituality (Mahwah, NJ: Paulist Press, 1982), 74.
3. See *A Sermon to Catechumens on the Creed* and chapter seven of *The Handbook on Faith, Hope, and Love* by Augustine of Hippo.
4. See *On Lent: VIII* by Leo the Great.
5. See *The Catechetical Lectures* by Cyril of Jerusalem.
6. There are numerous sermons and commentaries on the Nicene and other historic Christian creeds. Two worth mentioning are *On the Apostles' Creed* by Rufinius and *The Creedal Homilies* by Quodvultdeus of Carthage.
7. The version of the Nicene Creed, or more accurately the Nicene-Constantinopolitan Creed, used throughout this book is published by the Orthodox Church in America (https://oca.org/orthodoxy/the-orthodox-faith/doctrine-scripture/the-symbol-of-faith/nicene-creed). While there are many other excellent English translations available, this version strikes what I believe to be the ideal balance between faithfulness to the historical text, readability, and accepted liturgical use.
8. Augustine of Hippo, *Commentary on the Lord's Sermon on the Mount with Seventeen Related Sermons*, ed. Hermigild Dressler, trans. Denis J. Kavanagh, vol. 11, The Fathers of the Church (Washington, DC: The Catholic University of America Press, 1951), 240.
9. Augustine of Hippo, "On the Creed: A Sermon to the Catechumens," in *St. Augustin: On the Holy Trinity, Doctrinal Treatises, Moral Treatises*, ed. Philip Schaff, trans. C. L. Cornish, vol. 3, A Select Library of the Nicene and Post-Nicene Fathers of the Christian Church, First Series (Buffalo, NY: Christian Literature Company, 1887), 369.
10. The Apostles' Creed first appears in the late fourth century but, according to tradition, it was composed after the descent of the Holy Spirit at Pentecost, with each of the Twelve Apostles contributing a single phrase or idea. The Athanasian Creed doesn't appear until the sixth century and was almost certainly not written by Athanasius, one of the key figures at the Council of Nicaea.
11. Philip Schaff and Henry Wace, eds., "The Synodal Letter," in *The Seven Ecumenical Councils*, trans. Henry R. Percival, vol. 14, A Select Library of the Nicene and Post-Nicene Fathers of the Christian Church, Second Series (New York: Charles Scribner's Sons, 1900), 54.
12. See Schaff, *The Seven Ecumenical Councils*, 3.
13. Leo the Great, "Sermons," 159.
14. Ibid., 159–160.
15. Rick Brannan et al., eds., *The Lexham English Septuagint* (Bellingham, WA: Lexham Press, 2012), Is 7:9.
16. Rufinius, "A Commentary on the Apostles' Creed," in *Theodoret, Jerome, Gennadius, and Rufinius: Historical Writings*, ed. Philip Schaff, vol. 3, Nicene and Post-Nicene Fathers, Second Series, (Grand Rapids: Christian Classics Ethereal Library, 2009), 1389.
17. Ibid.
18. See Daniel 6:23.
19. See Genesis 17:17 and Romans 4:18.
20. See Mark 5:36-43.
21. G.K. Chesterton, *St. Francis of Assisi* (London: Hodder and Stoughton, 1923), 14.
22. Ibid., 14.

23 Rufinius, "A Commentary on the Apostles' Creed," 1391.
24 See Philippians 4:19.
25 See Isaiah 26:3.
26 See Proverbs 21:1.
27 See Genesis 18:1-21 and Hebrews 13:2.
28 Augustine of Hippo, "Concerning Faith of Things Not Seen," in *St. Augustin: On the Holy Trinity, Doctrinal Treatises, Moral Treatises*, ed. Philip Schaff, trans. C. L. Cornish, vol. 3, A Select Library of the Nicene and Post-Nicene Fathers of the Christian Church, First Series (Buffalo, NY: Christian Literature Company, 1887), 337.
29 See Genesis 3:6.
30 Cyprian of Carthage, "On the Lord's Prayer," in *Fathers of the Third Century: Hippolytus, Cyprian, Novatian, Appendix*, ed. Alexander Roberts, James Donaldson, and A. Cleveland Coxe, trans. Robert Ernest Wallis, vol. 5, The Ante-Nicene Fathers (Buffalo, NY: Christian Literature Company, 1886), 451.
31 Ibid.
32 Ibid.
33 See 2 Corinthians 4:7.
34 John Chrysostom, "Homilies of St. John Chrysostom, Archbishop of Constantinople, on the Epistle to the Hebrews," in *Saint Chrysostom: Homilies on the Gospel of St. John and Epistle to the Hebrews*, ed. Philip Schaff, trans. T. Keble and Frederic Gardiner, vol. 14, A Select Library of the Nicene and Post-Nicene Fathers of the Christian Church, First Series (New York: Christian Literature Company, 1889), 468.
35 See Matthew 14:29-30.
36 Dietrich Bonhoeffer, *Discipleship*, ed. Victoria J. Barnett, trans. Barbara Green and Reinhard Krauss, Reader's Edition, Dietrich Bonhoeffer Works (Minneapolis, MN: Fortress Press, 2015), 18–19.
37 Chrysostom, *Homilies on the Gospel of St. John and Epistle to the Hebrews*, 463.
38 See Acts 15:1-29.
39 See 1 Corinthians 8:1-13.
40 See Hebrews 13:8.
41 Rufinius, "A Commentary on the Apostles' Creed," 1390.
42 See Ephesians 2:8.
43 Cassius Dio, *Roman History*, trans. Earnest Cary, vol. 3, Loeb Classical Library (Cambridge: Harvard University Press, 1925), 63:5.3.
44 See Matthew 10:25.
45 See Matthew 25:34.
46 See 1 Peter 5:4.
47 John Cassian, "The Conferences of John Cassian," in *Sulpitius Severus, Vincent of Lérins, John Cassian*, ed. Philip Schaff and Henry Wace, trans. Edgar C. S. Gibson, vol. 11, A Select Library of the Nicene and Post-Nicene Fathers of the Christian Church, Second Series (New York: Christian Literature Company, 1894), 407.
48 A. J. Wensinck with Isaac of Nineveh, *Mystic Treatises* (Amsterdam: Koninklijke Akademie Van Wetenschappen, 1923), 227.
49 See John 9:35-36.
50 See Isaiah 55:9.

51 Gregory Palamas, *Gregory Palamas: The Triads*, ed. Richard J. Payne and John Meyendorff, trans. Nicholas Gendle, The Classics of Western Spirituality (Mahwah, NJ: Paulist Press, 1983), 32.

52 See Romans 11:33.

53 Oswald Chambers, *The Love of God* (Hants UK: Marshall, Morgan & Scott, 1996).

54 Hilary of Poitiers, "On the Trinity," in *St. Hilary of Poitiers, John of Damascus*, ed. Philip Schaff and Henry Wace, trans. E. W. Watson et al., vol. 9a, A Select Library of the Nicene and Post-Nicene Fathers of the Christian Church, Second Series (New York: Christian Literature Company, 1899), 42.

55 Ibid., 45.

56 St Gregory of Nazianzus, *On God and Christ: The Five Theological Orations and Two Letters to Cledonius*, ed. John Behr, trans. Frederick Williams and Lionel Wickham, Popular Patristics Series (Crestwood, NY: St Vladimir's Seminary Press, 2002), 118.

57 Ibid.

58 Gregory Nazianzen, "Select Orations of Saint Gregory Nazianzen," in *S. Cyril of Jerusalem, S. Gregory Nazianzen*, ed. Philip Schaff and Henry Wace, trans. Charles Gordon Browne and James Edward Swallow, vol. 7, A Select Library of the Nicene and Post-Nicene Fathers of the Christian Church, Second Series (New York: Christian Literature Company, 1894), 355.

59 Francis Schaeffer, *The Mark of the Christian* (Downers Grove: InterVarsity Press, 1970), 53.

60 Ibid., 52.

61 See Matthew 17:6.

62 See 2 Corinthians 4:6.

63 See Galatians 2:9.

64 See Mark 9:3.

65 See John 1:14, 8:12.

66 Palamas, *The Triads*, 37.

67 Ambrose of Milan, *The Letters of S. Ambrose, Bishop of Milan*, trans. H. Walford, A Library of Fathers of the Holy Catholic Church (London; Oxford; Cambridge: Oxford; James Parker and Co.; Rivingtons, 1881), 316.

68 See 2 Corinthians 8:3-7.

69 See 2 Peter 3:18.

70 See Philippians 2:7.

71 See 2 Corinthians 6:2.

72 Joel C. Elowsky, ed., John 1-10, *Ancient Christian Commentary on Scripture* (Downers Grove, IL: InterVarsity Press, 2006), 235.

73 Steven A. McKinion, ed., Isaiah 1-39, *Ancient Christian Commentary on Scripture* (Downers Grove, IL: InterVarsity Press, 2004), 100.

74 See Revelation 10:10.

75 Leo the Great, "Sermons," 140.

76 Ignatius of Antioch, "The Epistle of Ignatius to the Magnesians," in *The Apostolic Fathers with Justin Martyr and Irenaeus*, ed. Alexander Roberts, James Donaldson, and A. Cleveland Coxe, vol. 1, The Ante-Nicene Fathers (Buffalo, NY: Christian Literature Company, 1885), 61.

77 "St. Patrick's Breastplate," Our Catholic Prayers, accessed May 27, 2019, https://www.ourcatholicprayers.com/st-patricks-breastplate.html

78 See Matthew 1:18 and Galatians 4:4.

79 See Matthew 21:18 and Luke 4:2.

80 See John 19:28.

81 See Acts 3:15 and 1 Corinthians 2:8.

82 Gregory Nazianzen, "Select Orations," 433.

83 Athanasius of Alexandria, *Athanasius: On the Incarnation of the Word of God*, trans. T. Herbert Bindley, Second Edition Revised (London: The Religious Tract Society, 1903), 67.

84 See Genesis 1:26-27.

85 Oswald Chambers, *Biblical Ethics* (Hants UK: Marshall, Morgan & Scott, 1947).

86 Ibid.

87 Ibid.

88 See Isaiah 7:14 and Matthew 1:23.

89 Cyprian of Carthage, "On the Lord's Prayer," 450.

90 Leo the Great, "Sermons," 129.

91 Hilary of Poitiers, "On the Trinity," 47.

92 John Damascene, *Writings*, ed. Hermigild Dressler, trans. Frederic H. Chase Jr., vol. 37, The Fathers of the Church (Washington, DC: The Catholic University of America Press, 1958), 280.

93 Gregory Nazianzen, "Select Orations," 203.

94 "DNA: Comparing Humans and Chimps," American Museum of Natural History, accessed on May 27, 2019, https://www.amnh.org/exhibitions/permanent-exhibitions/anne-and-bernard-spitzer-hall-of-human-origins/understanding-our-past/dna-comparing-humans-and-chimps

95 Tertullian, "On the Resurrection of the Flesh," in *Latin Christianity: Its Founder, Tertullian*, ed. Alexander Roberts, James Donaldson, and A. Cleveland Coxe, trans. Peter Holmes, vol. 3, The Ante-Nicene Fathers (Buffalo, NY: Christian Literature Company, 1885), 549.

96 Athanasius, *On the Incarnation of the Word of God*, 69.

97 Gregory Zaiens, *O Full of Grace Glory to Thee*, ed. David C. Straut (South Canaan, PA: New Zadonsk Press, 2008), 1.

98 A.T. Robertson, *Word Pictures in the New Testament* (Nashville, TN: Broadman Press, 1933), Lk 1:28.

99 The Revised Standard Version (1994), the Douay-Rheims Bible (2009), and The Eastern/Greek Orthodox Bible: New Testament (2011) all read "full of grace" in Luke 1:28.

100 See John of Damascus (*Exposition of the Orthodox Faith*, 3.2), Origen (*Homilies on Luke*, 6.7), and Augustine (*The Enchiridion*, 36).

101 Ambrose of Milan, "Three Books of St. Ambrose on the Holy Spirit," in *St. Ambrose: Select Works and Letters*, ed. Philip Schaff and Henry Wace, trans. H. de Romestin, E. de Romestin, and H. T. F. Duckworth, vol. 10, A Select Library of the Nicene and Post-Nicene Fathers of the Christian Church, Second Series (New York: Christian Literature Company, 1896), 104.

102 See Isaiah 7:14.

103 Steven A. McKinion, ed., Isaiah 1-39, *Ancient Christian Commentary on Scripture* (Downers Grove, IL: InterVarsity Press, 2004), 63.

104 See 1 Samuel 6:19 and 2 Samuel 6:5-10.

105 Leo the Great, "Sermons," 129.

106 John Climacus, *The Ladder of Divine Ascent*, 74.

107 Augustine of Hippo, "The Enchiridion," in *St. Augustin: On the Holy Trinity, Doctrinal Treatises, Moral Treatises*, ed. Philip Schaff, trans. J. F. Shaw, vol. 3, A Select Library of the Nicene and Post-Nicene Fathers of the Christian Church, First Series (Buffalo, NY: Christian Literature Company, 1887), 248.

108 Leo the Great, "Sermons," 131.

109 Dallas Willard, "Live Life to the Full," *Christian Herald*, April 14, 2001, accessed May 27, 2019, http://www.dwillard.org/articles/individual/live-life-to-the-full

110 See Luke 1:35.

111 John Chrysostom, "The Nativity Sermon of St. John Chrysostom," Antiochian Orthodox Christian Archdiocese of North America, accessed on May 29, 2019, http://ww1.antiochian.org/node/21955

112 See John 8:3-11.

113 Dallas Willard, "Live Life to the Full"

114 Ibid.

115 Mark S. Brocker, "Editor's Introduction to the English Edition," in *Conspiracy and Imprisonment: 1940–1945*, ed. Jørgen Glenthøj, Ulrich Kabitz, and Wolf Krötke, trans. Lisa E. Dahill and Douglas W. Stott, vol. 16 (Minneapolis, MN: Fortress Press, 2006), 1.

116 Dietrich Bonhoeffer, *Conspiracy and Imprisonment: 1940–1945*, ed. Jørgen Glenthøj et al., trans. Lisa E. Dahill and Douglas W. Stott, vol. 16 (Minneapolis, MN: Fortress Press, 2006), 470.

117 Dietrich Bonhoeffer, *Discipleship*, 196.

118 The phrase "one of the Trinity suffered in the flesh" is an often-repeated simplification of a statement made by the Fifth Ecumenical Council, "If anyone does not confess that our Lord Jesus Christ who was crucified in the flesh is true God and the Lord of Glory and one of the Holy Trinity: let him be anathema" (Schaff, *The Seven Ecumenical Councils*, 314). For more on this subject, see *The Suffering of the Impassible God: The Dialectics of Patristic Thought* by Paul L. Gavrilyuk, published by Oxford University Press.

119 Dietrich Bonhoeffer, *Discipleship*, 196.

120 Ignatius of Antioch, "The Epistle of Ignatius to the Romans," in *The Apostolic Fathers with Justin Martyr and Irenaeus*, ed. Alexander Roberts, James Donaldson, and A. Cleveland Coxe, vol. 1, The Ante-Nicene Fathers (Buffalo, NY: Christian Literature Company, 1885), 76.

121 Ibid.

122 See Acts 11:26.

123 Ibid.

124 Vassilios Papavassiliou, *Meditations for Advent: Preparing for Christ's Birth* (Chesterton, IN: Ancient Faith Publishing, 2013), 106–107.

125 Martin Hengle, *Crucifixion*, (Philadelphia, PA: Fortress Press, 1977), 33.

126 Ibid.

127 Irenaeus of Lyons, "Irenæus against Heresies," in *The Apostolic Fathers with Justin Martyr and Irenaeus*, ed. Alexander Roberts, James Donaldson, and A. Cleveland Coxe, vol. 1, The Ante-Nicene Fathers (Buffalo, NY: Christian Literature Company, 1885), 447.

128 John Damascene, *Writings*, 319–320.

129 John Henry Newman, *Parochial and Plain Sermons*, vol. 1 (London; Oxford; Cambridge: Rivingtons, 1868), 67.

130 Dietrich Bonhoeffer, *Discipleship*, 196.

131 Ibid., 202.

132 Tertullian, "Ad Martyres," in *Latin Christianity: Its Founder, Tertullian*, ed. Alexander Roberts, James Donaldson, and A. Cleveland Coxe, trans. S. Thelwall, vol. 3, The Ante-Nicene Fathers (Buffalo, NY: Christian Literature Company, 1885), 704.

133 Chrysostom, *Homilies on the Gospel of St. John and Epistle to the Hebrews*, 489.

134 Ignatius of Antioch, *The Letters: English Translation*, ed. John Behr, trans. Alistair Stewart, vol. 49, Popular Patristics Series (Yonkers, NY: St Vladimir's Seminary Press, 2013), 91.

135 See Acts 2:22-36.

136 See Acts 13:35-37.

137 See Cyril of Alexandria (Letter 11a), Augustine (*The City of God*, 27.2), and John of Damascus (*Exposition of the Orthodox Faith*, 3.28).

138 Hilary of Poitiers, "On the Trinity," 44.

139 Leo the Great, "Sermons," 189.

140 Tertullian, "On the Resurrection of the Flesh," 561.

141 Augustine of Hippo, "On the Trinity," in *St. Augustin: On the Holy Trinity, Doctrinal Treatises, Moral Treatises*, ed. Philip Schaff, trans. Arthur West Haddan, vol. 3, A Select Library of the Nicene and Post-Nicene Fathers of the Christian Church, First Series (Buffalo, NY: Christian Literature Company, 1887), 72.

142 Gregory of Nyssa, "Gregory of Nyssa against Eunomius," in *Gregory of Nyssa: Dogmatic Treatises*, Etc., ed. Philip Schaff and Henry Wace, trans. William Moore et al., vol. 5, A Select Library of the Nicene and Post-Nicene Fathers of the Christian Church, Second Series (New York: Christian Literature Company, 1893), 113.

143 Ibid.

144 John Damascene, *Writings*, 350.

145 Athanasius, *On the Incarnation of the Word of God*, 142.

146 Joel C. Elowsky, ed., John 11–21, Ancient Christian Commentary on Scripture (Downers Grove, IL: InterVarsity Press, 2007), 354.

147 John Climacus, *The Ladder of Divine Ascent*, 179.

148 John Chrysostom, "Homilies of St. John Chrysostom, Archbishop of Constantinople, on the Epistle of St. Paul to the Romans," in *Saint Chrysostom: Homilies on the Acts of the Apostles and the Epistle to the Romans*, ed. Philip Schaff, trans. J. B. Morris, W. H. Simcox, and George B. Stevens, vol. 11, A Select Library of the Nicene and Post-Nicene Fathers of the Christian Church, First Series (New York: Christian Literature Company, 1889), 405.

149 Ibid.

150 St. John Chysostom, quoted in George Florovsky, "And Ascended Into Heaven...," *Orthodox Church in America*, accessed June 9, 2019, http://oca.org/saints/all-lives/2021/06/10

151 John Damascene, *Writings*, 350.

152 Leo the Great, "Sermons," 143.

153 St. Tikhon's Seminary. *Orthodox Daily Prayers*. St. Tikhon's Seminary Press, 1982. Print.

154 Chrysostom, "The Nativity Sermon"

155 St. Augustine of Hippo, "Ascension of Christ – Augustine," *Crossroads Initiative*, accessed June 9, 2019, https://www.crossroadsinitiative.com/saints/ascension_of_christ_augustine/

156 Ibid.

157 Leo the Great, "Sermons," 160.

158 Cyprian of Carthage, "On Jealousy and Envy," in *Fathers of the Third Century: Hippolytus, Cyprian, Novatian*, Appendix, ed. Alexander Roberts, James Donaldson, and A. Cleveland Coxe, trans. Robert Ernest Wallis, vol. 5, The Ante-Nicene Fathers (Buffalo, NY: Christian Literature Company, 1886), 495.

159 Arthur A. Just, ed., Luke, *Ancient Christian Commentary on Scripture* (Downers Grove, IL: InterVarsity Press, 2005), 270.

160 John Cassian, *John Cassian: Conferences*, ed. John Farina, trans. Colm Luibheid, The Classics of Western Spirituality (New York; Mahwah, NJ: Paulist Press, 1985), 39.

161 Ibid., 39-41.

162 Ibid.

163 Ibid., 40.

164 Ambrose, "Three Books of St. Ambrose on the Holy Spirit," 120.

165 Ibid., 118.

166 St Gregory of Nazianzus, *Festal Orations*, ed. John Behr, trans. Nonna Verna Harrison, vol. 36, Popular Patristics Series (Crestwood, NY: St Vladimir's Seminary Press, 2008), 94.

167 See Athanasius, *On the Incarnation of the Word of God*, 142.

168 See S. Augustine, *Homilies on the Gospel according to St. John, and His First Epistle: Hom. 1-124, S. John 1-21 and Hom. 1-10, 1 S. John*, vol. 1 & 2, A Library of Fathers of the Holy Catholic Church, Anterior to the Division of the East and West: Translated by Members of the English Church (Oxford; London: John Henry Parker; F. and J. Rivington, 1848-1849), 643.

169 See John Damascene, *Writings*, 378-379.

170 See John 4:16-18.

171 Cyril of Jerusalem, "The Catechetical Lectures of S. Cyril, Archbishop of Jerusalem," in *S. Cyril of Jerusalem, S. Gregory Nazianzen*, ed. Philip Schaff and Henry Wace, trans. R. W. Church and Edwin Hamilton Gifford, vol. 7, A Select Library of the Nicene and Post-Nicene Fathers of the Christian Church, Second Series (New York: Christian Literature Company, 1894), 118.

172 Steven A. McKinion, ed., Isaiah 1-39, *Ancient Christian Commentary on Scripture* (Downers Grove, IL: InterVarsity Press, 2004), 100.

173 See Luke 23:34.

174 Cyril of Jerusalem, "The Catechetical Lectures," 118.

175 Gregory of Nazianzus, *Festal Orations*, 94.

176 Ambrose, "Three Books of St. Ambrose on the Holy Spirit," 103.

177 Cyril of Jerusalem, *Lectures on the Christian Sacraments: The Procatechesis and the Five Mystagogical Catecheses*, ed. F. L. Cross and John Behr, Popular Patristics Series, Number 2 (Crestwood, NY: St Vladimir's Seminary Press, 1977), 40-41.

178 Gregory of Nazianzus, *Festal Orations*, 94.

179 See Acts 9:18.

180 See Matthew 3:13-17.

181 St. John Cassian, "On the Holy Fathers of Sketis," trans. G.E.H. Palmer, Philip Sherrard, Kallistos Ware, vol. 1, *The Philokalia* (New York: Farrar, Straus and Giroux, 1979), 107.

182 Gregory of Nazianzus, *Festal Orations*, 106-107.

183 John Chrysostom, "Homilies on Genesis 18-45," ed. Thomas P. Halton, trans. Robert C. Hill, vol. 82, *The Fathers of the Church* (Washington, DC: The Catholic University of America Press, 1990), 83.

184 Ibid.

185 Augustine, "On the Trinity," 72.

186 John Damascene, *Writings*, 401.

187 Cyril of Jerusalem, "The Catechetical Lectures," 139.

188 Hilary of Poitiers, "On the Trinity," 215.

189 Leo the Great, "Sermons," 204.

190 Cyril of Jerusalem, *The Catechetical Lectures of S. Cyril* (Oxford; London: John Henry Parker; J. G. and F. Rivington, 1838), 253.

191 John Climacus, *The Ladder of Divine Ascent*, 91.

192 Ibid., 132.

193 Ibid.

194 Billy Graham, "You Can Have Resurrection Life: A Classic Message from Billy Graham," Billy Graham Evangelistic Association, accessed on May 27, 2019, https://billygraham.org/decision-magazine/april-2017/can-resurrection-life-classic-message-billy-graham

195 John Climacus, *The Ladder of Divine Ascent*, 274.

196 Ibid., 278.

197 G.K. Chesterton, *St. Francis of Assisi*, 139.

ACKNOWLEDGMENTS

While my name is on the cover of this book, it seems wrong to call myself its author. I acted chiefly as a compiler—drawing from those first great Christians who communicated the faith with such beauty and depth that my most significant contribution was staying out of the way. To the fathers at the Council of Nicaea and all who followed in their steps, I pray your words retain the same force in this abbreviated form that they did for me unabridged.

On this side of eternity, there are countless pastors, friends, and family members to whom I owe my gratitude for reading drafts and providing encouragement and correction along the way. But since it is impossible to list them all, I will mention four whose contributions made this book a reality.

Thank you, David, for gently guiding every step of this process and for encouraging me to stop and ponder the mystery of God becoming flesh.

Thank you, James, for talking through so many half-baked ideas and for your unwavering friendship.

Thank you, Kathy, for reading, re-reading, and providing feedback on almost every word.

Thank you, Jacqueline, for your patient love and for posing the question all those years ago to which this book is a partial and ever-unfolding answer.

THE BOOK CONTINUES AT:
POWEROFTHECREED.COM

with videos,

podcasts,

study guides,

and more

by Mark Nauroth.

COMMENTS OR QUESTIONS?

You can contact Mark at
info@powerofthecreed.com

Made in the USA
Coppell, TX
05 September 2020